MONET

IN HOLLAND

MONET
IN HOLLAND

UITGEVERIJ WAANDERS, ZWOLLE

RIJKSMUSEUM VINCENT VAN GOGH, AMSTERDAM
in cooperation with the Municipal Archives, Amsterdam

The following helped to make the exhibition *Monet in Holland* possible:

This book is published to coincide with the exhibition, *Monet in Holland*, at the Rijksmuseum Vincent van Gogh, Amsterdam, from 17 October 1986 to 4 January 1987.

ISBN 90 6630 079 5 (bounded)
99 6630 072 8 (paperback)

Design: Roelof Koebrugge GVN in cooperation with
Mischa Bense, Publicis Intermarco
Editor: Louis van Tilborgh

Cover: Claude Monet, *Zaandam: Houses on the Achterzaan*, 1872.
Metropolitan Museum of Art, Robert Lehman Collection, New York
Letter Claude Monet to Camille Pissarro, 2 juni 1871.
From: Daniel Wildenstein, *Claude Monet: Biographie et catalogue raisonné*, Lausanne & Paris 1974, p. 427.

Page 2:   Claude Monet, *Bulb-fields and mills near Rijnsburg*.
The Hague, Rijksdienst Beeldende Kunst, on loan to the Stedelijk Museum, Amsterdam.

CONTENT

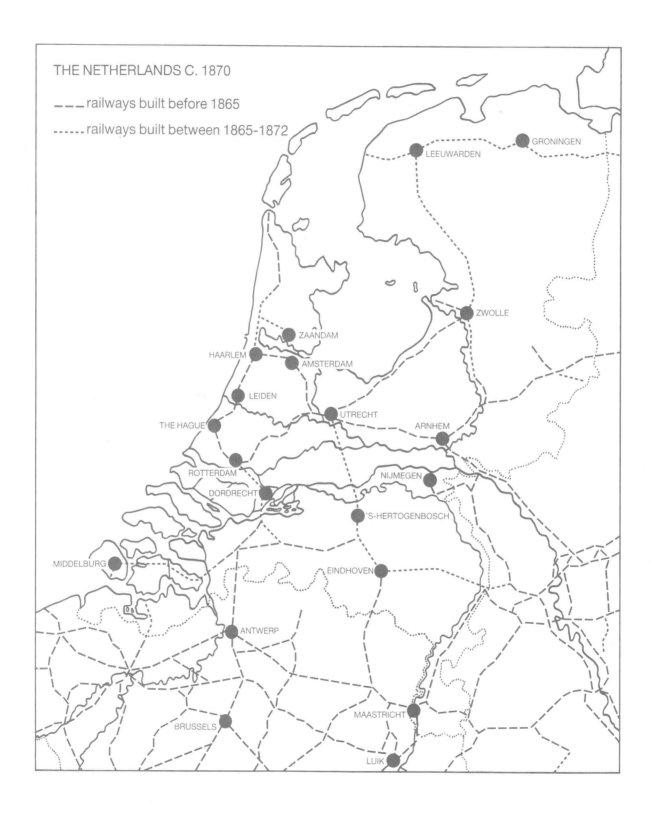

THE NETHERLANDS C. 1870

_ _ _ railways built before 1865

.... railways built between 1865-1872

GRONINGEN

LEEUWARDEN

ZWOLLE

ZAANDAM

HAARLEM

AMSTERDAM

LEIDEN

UTRECHT

THE HAGUE

ARNHEM

ROTTERDAM

NIJMEGEN

DORDRECHT

'S-HERTOGENBOSCH

MIDDELBURG

EINDHOVEN

ANTWERP

BRUSSELS

MAASTRICHT

LUIK

PREFACE

Monet's visits to Holland, the last of which took place exactly one hundred years ago this year, have suffered from constant underexposure in the literature on Impressionism. That Monet planted his easel not only in Honfleur, Argenteuil and Giverny, but also on the banks of the Zaan, by the Amsterdam canals and in the midst of the colourful bulb-fields between Leiden and Haarlem has frequently gone unnoticed, in spite of the resulting yield of more than forty paintings. This may have been caused by the fact that a large proportion of these are privately owned, and thus less accessible. Monet's persistent inclusion of his Dutch work in exhibitions can be seen as attesting to the weight he attached to it himself. Thus he opened his submissions to the fourth Impressionist group exhibition in 1879 with his *Habitation bourgeoise, à Zaandum (Hollande)*. The experience which the 'Raphael of water' acquired in painting views of the Zaan can be seen in some of his representations of the Seine at Argenteuil. It is not surprising, then, that such a Zaan canvas was regarded until recently as being French. The attention Monet later paid to the bulb-fields also seems to have proved a useful lesson for his depictions of luxuriant flower-fields in the mid-1880s.

During his final visit to Holland, in 1886, Monet mentioned in passing that he had been there several times before. How often he painted in the Netherlands between 1871 and 1886 - one of the blank spaces in Monet's biography - has unfortunately remained a mystery for the compilers of this exhibition. He certainly must have been here on at least one other occasion in the 1870s, as perusal of the weather reports teaches us: Monet cannot have painted his two Amsterdam snow scenes during the 1871 stay. Style and painting technique also supply sufficient indications that the Zaan views and most of the Amsterdam paintings may not be assigned to the same year. Hopefully, the concentration of so many Dutch paintings at this exhibition will bring the specialists closer to solving the problem.

Boudewijn Bakker, curator of the Amsterdam Municipal Archives, was the originator of the plan for an exhibition on 'Monet in Holland'. He was also largely responsible for devising the exhibition, and the topographical research carried out both by him and, under his direction, by Marijke de Groot, led to countless refinements on the identification of places depicted by Monet. Furthermore, as the writer of the opening article, he provides a vivid delineation of the cultural climate of the time, in the context of which Monet's Dutch travels should be seen. I am most grateful to both him and to Dr. W.Chr. Pieterse, Municipal Archivist in Amsterdam, for the time and energy he has been able to invest in this co-operative venture involving our two institutions. The Municipal Archives has also had an invaluable rôle as a lender to the exhibition.

The other authors, too, have been no mean contributors towards the making of the exhibition. Ernst van de Wetering, attached to the Central Laboratory for Research on Objects of Art and Science in Amsterdam, has applied himself to penetrating more deeply into the essence of the Impressionist art of painting, even when an occasional popular myth has had to be disfigured along the way. Joop Joosten, Stedelijk Museum Amsterdam, places Monet's 'discovery' of a pile of Japanese prints against the background of the age-old ties between Japan and Holland. A.H. Huusen, professor of history at the University of Groningen, who has published work on Monet's stay in Holland before, writes here on the political background to Monet's journey to London and Holland. Finally, Ronald Pickvance publishes and annotates a number of documents which shed new light on the rôle of Theo van Gogh as Monet's art-dealer in the late 1880s. By kind courtesy of the Vincent van Gogh Foundation, it has also been possible to publish here, for the first time and within a suitable context, letters written by Claude Monet to Theo, as well as fragments from the letters from Theo to his fiancée, later his wife Jo Bonger.

Ronald Pickvance's familiarity with Monet's oeuvre, consolidated over many years, makes him the obvious person to furnish the individual works with informative notes. Although not all the paintings are at the exhibition, the choice has been to catalogue Monet's

Dutch oeuvre as a whole. We can follow the artist's steps on all his excursions. For this purpose Marijke de Groot and Boudewijn Bakker have assembled a large amount of comparative topographical material. They were greatly supported in this endeavour by J.D. Bakker at Zaandam, J. Zonjee, until recently Municipal Archivist for Zaanstad, and the present staff of the Amsterdam Municipal Archives.

The final editing of the catalogue was in the capable hands of Louis van Tilborgh, staff member of the exhibition department of the Van Gogh Museum. On his shoulders, and on those of the designer Mischa Bense, rested the burden of producing the publication in time, in spite of the usual stretching of all the deadlines. Waanders of Zwolle Ltd., both their Publishing Company and the Printers respectively, share the credit for having produced an extremely attractive publication which we hope will appeal to both a specialised readership and to a broader section of the general public.

The detective work undertaken by the compilers of the exhibition in order to discover the whereabouts of some of Monet's works was very time-consuming and laborious. It has not been successful in every case, but nevertheless, twenty-three of Monet's Dutch works were able to return temporarily to their country of origin. The majority of the remaining paintings could at least be reproduced by means of recent photographs. A number of works were not available for the exhibition on account of donation conditions, and some others were in too poor a state to journey to Amsterdam. However, a gratifyingly large number of owners reacted generously to our applications for loans. With gratitude, their names are mentioned separately, elsewhere in the catalogue, except in cases where such mention was declined. Also listed are the names of those who lent works by Monet's contemporaries for the exhibition. For Monet's work is flanked by a selection from both French and Dutch contemporaries, who were fascinated by the Dutch landscape and the town views. The exhibition opens with work by Corot, Ziem, Daubigny, Manet, Boudin, Jongkind and Guillaumin who, just as Monet, journeyed northwards to visit and to paint the land of Rembrandt. Apart from them we have chosen Dutch artists of the last quarter of the nineteenth century, whose paintings present us in some cases with interesting parallels with Monet's work, and in others with instructive contrasts. In this connection it was certainly a most apt discovery that Vincent van Gogh himself, later a fervent admirer of Monet, was one of the rare artists before Monet, to choose the brightly-coloured bulb-fields as a subject. I am immensely grateful to Mr. J. Carter Brown, Director of the National Gallery of Art in Washington, for his willingness to part with this painting, so recently acquired by his museum, for this occasion.

Countless people have supported us in word and deed, conducted investigations or mediated in obtaining loans, of these I can only mention a selected number. It goes without saying that our gratitude also extends to their immediate staff. They are: William Acquavella, Acquavella Galleries, New York; Steve Austen, Director Netherlands Theatre Institute, Amsterdam; William Beadleston, William Beadleston, Inc., New York; Robert P. Bergman, Director, Walters Art Gallery, Baltimore; Charles E. van Blommestein, formerly Acting Director Rijksmuseum Vincent van Gogh, Amsterdam; Ivo Bouwman, The Hague; H. Bronkhorst, Baarn; B. Buijze, Institut Néerlandais, Paris; Françoise Cachin, Director, Musée d'Orsay, Paris; Martha op de Coul, Department of 19th-century Dutch and Belgian Art, Rijksbureau voor Kunsthistorische Dokumentatie, The Hague; Tony Daalder, Stedelijk Museum, Amsterdam; France Daguet, Durand-Ruel & Cie, Paris; Petra J.T. ten Doesschate-Chu, South Orange, New Jersey; Job R.Q. van Dooren, The Hague; E.G. Duyvis, Heiloo; K.N.M.I., De Bilt; E. Glasbergen-Duyvis, Diever; Caroline Godfroy, Durand-Ruel & Cie, Paris; Johan van Gogh, Chairman Vincent van Gogh Foundation, Amsterdam; Robert Gordon, New York; Robert R. de Haas, Director Rijksdienst Beeldende Kunst, The Hague; Stephen Hahn, New York; Lynn W. Hanke, Acquavella Galleries, New York; Carlos van Hasselt, Director Fondation Custodia, Paris; Paulien van der Heide, Museum voor de Bloembol-

8

lenstreek, Lisse; Professor John House, Courtauld Institute (University of London); Ay Wang Hsia, Wildenstein and Company, New York; William R. Johnston, Assistant Director, Walters Art Gallery, Baltimore; Mariette Josephus Jitta, Curator of Prints, Haags Gemeentemuseum, The Hague; Nathan Kernan, Robert Miller Galleries, New York; Hans Kraan, Head of the International Department, Rijksbureau voor Kunsthistorische Dokumentatie, The Hague; Willem Laanstra, Zaandam; Michel Laclotte, Inspector General of the French National Museums, Paris; Suzanne G. Lindsay, Philadelphia; Laura Lucky, The Shelburne Museum Inc., Shelburne; G.J. Luyendijk, Amsterdam; Marlborough Fine Art, Londen; Mr. and Mrs. Paul Mellon, Washington; Robert Miller, Robert Miller Galleries, New York; Philippe de Montebello, Director Metropolitan Museum of Art, New York; Alexandra R. Murphy, Sterling and Francine Clark Art Institute, Williamstown; Constance Pemberton, Sotheby's, London; Dr. R.W.D. Oxenaar, Director, Rijksmuseum Kröller-Müller, Otterlo; Willem Rappard, Head Department of 19th-century Dutch and Belgian Art, Rijksbureau voor Kunsthistorische Dokumentatie, The Hague; Alex Reid & Lefevre Art Gallery, London; Joseph Rishel, Curator, Philadelphia Museum of Art and The John G. Johnson Collection, Philadelphia; J.H.H. van Roosmalen, Tilburg; Mrs. Th. van Royen, Netherlands Embassy, Lisbon; C.W. van Scherpenzeel, K.N.M.I., De Bilt; Robert Schmit, Paris; Th.P.G. Snelting, Eindhoven; Michel Strauss, Department of Impressionist and Modern Paintings, Sotheby's, London; John L. Tancock, Department of Impressionist and Modern Paintings, Sotheby's, New York; Mrs. J.Th. Tavera, Musée Marmottan, Paris; Eugene V. Thaw, E.V. Thaw and Company, New York; J.P. Vooren, Zaandam; Daniel Wildenstein, Fondation Wildenstein, Paris; Eric Zaffran, Curator, Walters Art Gallery, Balti-

more; W.M. Alberts, E.O. van der Goot and P.H.J. Vlasveld, Municipal Archives Amsterdam; C. den Dunnen and Titia de Groot, Municipal Archives Zaanstad.

Thanks are also due, of course, to all the staff members of the Rijksmuseum Vincent van Gogh, who have exerted themselves to make this exhibition possible. I extend thanks to Han van Crimpen and his staff of the conservation and documentation department. Dirk van der Oord was in charge of public relations. Henk Douna and Loud van Leeuwen coordinated transport operations and the installation of the exhibition. Marijke de Groot, with the secretarial assistance of Inger Kreemer, conducted the voluminous correspondence.

How often is it not their fate that excellent ideas for exhibitions find a quiet grave as soon as the first obstacle, usually of a financial nature, is encountered. Happily, rather than being doomed to remain a reconstruction on paper only, one hundred years after Monet's last visit to our country it has been possible to reunite a large part of Monet's Dutch oeuvre. That this has been realised is not only thanks to the generosity of the owners and the exertions of the scholars, but in the final instance also to the cooperative efforts of government and industry. In addition to liberal contributions made by the Ministry of Welfare, Public Health and Culture, the sponsorship of Publicis-Intermarco has helped to make *Monet in Holland* come about. As the chief sponsor of *La France aux Pays-Bas*, the two-year long manifestation of which *Monet in Holland* is the final event, Credit Lyonnais deserves especial mention here. The Rijksmuseum Vincent van Gogh hopes to make many simular contributions to Dutch-French cultural relations in the years to come.

Ronald de Leeuw
Director
Rijksmuseum Vincent van Gogh

LENDERS TO THE EXHIBITION

Amsterdam
Municipal Archives
Rijksprentenkabinet
Stedelijk Museum

Baltimore
The Walters Art Gallery

Bordeaux
Musée des Beaux-Arts

Brussels
Collection d'Arschot

Cambridge
Syndics of the Fitzwilliam Museum

Douai
Musée de la Chartreuse

Groningen
Groninger Museum,
Foundation J.B. Scholten Fonds

Haarlem
Municipal Archives
Teylers Museum

The Hague
Algemeen Rijksarchief
Art Gallery Ivo Bouwman B.V.
Haags Gemeentemuseum
Rijksdienst Beeldende Kunst

Houston
The Museum of Fine Arts,
John A. and Audrey Jones Beck Collection

Laren (NH)
Singer Museum

Lisbon
Calouste Gulbenkian Museum

Macon
Musée des Ursulines

New York
The Metropolitan Museum of Art,
Robert Lehman Collection

Otterlo
Rijksmuseum Kröller-Müller

Oxford
The Visitors of the Ashmolean Museum

Paris
Musée d'Orsay
Galerie Schmit

Philadelphia
Philadelphia Museum of Art,
W.P. Wilstach Collection

Rotterdam
Museum Boymans-van Beuningen

Stockholm
Nationalmuseum

Swansea
Glynn Vivian Art Gallery and Museum

United States
William Kelly Simpson
Collection Henry Ford II

Utrecht
Centraal Museum

Washington
National Gallery of Art,
Collection Mr. and Mrs. Paul Mellon

Wiliamstown, Mass.
Sterling and Francine Clark Art Institiute

Zaandam
Municipal Archives Zaanstad

Anonymous lenders

Detail: Claude Monet, *The Dam and the locks on the Achterzaan.* Private collection.

CHRONOLOGY

1840   14 November: Oscar-Claude Monet born in Parijs.

1858   Monet becomes acquainted with Boudin and is first introduced to painting in the open air.

1860   The young artist attends classes at the Académie Suisse in Parijs.

1862   After a year's military service in Algeria, Monet makes the acquaintance of Jongkind in Le Havre.

1864   Monet, together with Jongkind and Boudin, paints sea views in Honfleur.

1865   Two paintings sent in by Monet are accepted by the Salon, and later the same year he submits them to the Amsterdam exhibition of works produced by living artists, being the Dutch equivalent of the French Salon.

1867   Jean Monet born, the son of Claude Monet and Camille Doncieux.

1870   After the declaration of war between Prussia and France the couple, now married, take refuge with their son Jean in London, where Monet meets Daubigny and the art-dealer Durand-Ruel.

1871   Monet leaves for Holland with his wife and child, arriving in Zaandam on 2 June. The painter stays until 8 October and after a short stay in Amsterdam he leaves for Paris. The exact date of his return journey is not known; it is only definite that Monet was back in Paris by 19 November.

1874   Monet is now living in Argenteuil. He exhibits his painting *Impression, Sunrise* at the first group exhibition of the 'Société anonyme des artistes peintres'.

1878   Alice Hoschedé and her children come to live with the Monet family in Vétheuil.

1879   Camille Monet dies at the age of 32.

1881-   Monet works variously in the sur-
1883   roundings of Vétheuil and on the Normandy coast.
The painter settles in Giverny with Alice Hoschedé and her children.

1884   On the coast of the Riviera Monet paints for months in the neighbourhood of Bordighera.

1886   From 27 April to 6 May Monet stays in The Hague in order to paint the bulb-fields by Oegstgeest and Sassenheim. This visit takes place at the invitation of Baron d'Estournelles de Constant, secretary of the French ambassador.

1888   Theo van Gogh shows Monet's work, being views of the Antibes coast, at the Gallery of Boussod and Valadon.

1890   Monet purchases the house in Giverny which he has been living in since 1883. The artist now begins to make several versions of one specific subject. Thus the *Haystacks* series and that of *Rouen Cathedral* come about.

1893   Monet buys a piece of land in Giverny and proceeds to put in the famous pond with water-lilies.

1899-   Monet goes to London, returning there
1904   during the following three years to work on the *Thames* series. Meanwhile the pond with water-lilies claims an ever greater portion of this attention.

1908   At the end of 1908 Monet stays in Venice for a few months, this visit also leading to a series.

1911   Alice Monet, Monet's legal wife since 1892, dies.

1914   Death of Monet's eldest son, Jean.

1916-   The painter has a special studio built in
1926   order to be able to work on the *Water-lilies*. In reaction to the Armistice he presents this series to the French state in 1918. On 5 December 1926 Monet dies in Giverny at the age of 86. One year later his *Water-lilies* series is transferred to the Paris Orangerie.

1. Gustave Fraipont, *Chemin de Fer du Nord, Hollande,* late nineteenth century. Amsterdam, Municipal Archives.

MONET AS A TOURIST*

Boudewijn Bakker

'My dear friend,
We have finally arrived at the end of our journey, after a rather unpleasant crossing. We traversed almost the whole length of Holland and, to be sure, what I saw of it seemed far more beautiful than it is said to be. Zaandam is particularly remarkable and there is enough to paint here for a lifetime: I believe we have found very good accommodation here. The Dutch seem most friendly and hospitable (...) The baby and my wife are very well now, after having been sorely troubled by seasickness.'[1]

These words were written by Claude Monet from 'Hotel de Beurs, Zaandam near Amsterdam, Holland' on 2 June 1871, to his friend, the painter Camille Pissarro.[2] One or two days before, the Monets had left London, where they had taken refuge, in common with Pissarro and so many other fellow-countrymen, when the Prussian army invaded France in the autumn of 1870. The Monets had apparently travelled by packet-boat from London to Rotterdam and then by train to Amsterdam. Every day there were a few ships leaving for Zaandam from the Amsterdam docks; one of these was 'De Prins van Oranje' which moored in front of the hotel and inn 'De Beurs', a few yards from the Dam (fig. 2). In this simple hotel the Monet family was installed in a room with a balcony overlooking the harbour bay and the Dam. Monet recorded the view both in his sketch-book and in a painting (fig. 3,4).

It evidently suited the painter very well to be staying in Zaandam, for he wrote in a second letter to Pissarro two weeks later, on 17 June: 'As far as we are concerned, we have very good accommodation here and shall remain here for the summer; then I may go to Paris, but for the moment there is work to be done, this is a super place for painting, there are the most amusing things everywhere. Houses of every colour, hundreds of windmills and enchanting boats, extremely friendly Dutchmen who almost all speak French. Moreover, the weather is very fine, so that I have already started on a number of canvasses. (...) I have not yet had time to visit the museums. What I want first of all is to work, and I shall allow myself all that later.'[3]

Monet did indeed go on painting in Zaandam, even longer than the whole summer. From the four months that he lived there, twenty-four paintings have been preserved, about half of which are views in the immediate surroundings of the hotel. Most of the others were also made in the village or just outside it. As far as we know Monet did not once put up his easel outside the town limits of Zaandam.

It was not until 8 October that Monet finally, 'accompanied by his wife and child, left by boat for Amsterdam, to continue his journey from there within a few days.'[4] No written record other than this one has been preserved of the visit to Amsterdam. At about 10 October Monet signed the visitors' book at the Frans Hals Museum in Haarlem, and he certainly must have been back in Paris before 19 November.[5] Similary to the Zaandam landscapes, the twelve-odd views of the city which Monet painted in Amsterdam also cover a limited area: all the locations are along the IJ or the Inner Amstel, within a ten-minute walk from the Montelbaans tower.

Both the Zaandam and the Amsterdam canvasses exhibit striking differences in style

2. Zaandam, *The harbour and the Dam; on the right hotel-café De Beurs*, c. 1870. Photo: Zaandam, Municipal Archives Zaanstad.

among themselves, which seems to indicate that Monet came here on more than one occasion. As far as Amsterdam is concerned it is certain, in any case, that not all the paintings were made in the autumn of 1871, as two of them are winter scenes with snow. However, there is not one written source alluding to a second or third stay in the 1870s. The only reference that we have is fifteen years later, in 1886, when Monet came to Holland for the last time, and there was a short article on this visit in the periodical *De Portefeuille*, noting that Monet 'had sojourned [here] (…) more than once before.'[6]

This last time, Monet went to see the bulbfields at the height of the tulip season, from 27 April to 6 May 1886. Two days after arriving he wrote to his friend Théodore Duret of 'enormous fields in full flower; they are quite admirable, but drive the poor painter mad; they cannot be rendered with our poor palette.'[7] Forty years later he still remembered suddenly seeing barges pass by full of cut 'tulip heads', the whole resembling 'rafts of colour, yellow patches that

came gliding along in the blue reflection of the sky.'[8]

Only in this last case do we know what prompted Monet to come to Holland: he had been invited by a French diplomat in The Hague, Baron d'Estournelles de Constant, whose brother had connections with the Paris art world. Apparently Monet's art dealer, Durand-Ruel, was also involved in the journey; not only did the painter inform him of his departure beforehand, but he also sent him a letter requesting the money to return home, a mere three days after having arrived.[9] With or without the mediation of Durand-Ruel, Monet actually sold his host a painting; as far as we know this was the only landscape for which he ever found a buyer in Holland (cat. no. 39).

Within Monet's oeuvre, his Dutch landscapes - the total number is more than forty - constitute a group which is not without importance but which has scarcely been studied and remains problematic. This is partly because we still have very little information as to the time

16

3. Claude Monet, *Interior*. Paris, Museé Marmottan.

and place of Monet's visits to Holland, and his reasons for undertaking them. The mere fact that he did not return directly to France in May 1870 is noteworthy, especially taking into account that Monet had hardly proved an adventurous traveller up to 1870. He was born in Paris in 1840, and - aside from one year's military service in Algeria - he spent the first thirty years of his life in the district between Paris and the mouth of the Seine, the area around Le Havre where he had grown up. The reasons behind Monet's departure for London in 1870 were not artistic but political and social. After his initial Dutch excursion(s) it was not until 1883 that he once more headed for regions far from home, this time the Riviera. And only then did Monet begin to travel with some regularity, to Holland, London, Norway, the Riviera and Venice.

Leaving aside the matter of the journey it-self, Monet's choice of places to visit within Holland also raises certain questions. The windmills along the River Zaan, the Amster-dam canals, the bulb-fields - it reads like the itinerary of a tourist's day trip. What was Mo-net actually looking for in Holland, and what made him light upon precisely these areas? Was it coincidence, intuition or tradition? Oddly enough, this question is either not posed in art-historical literature or it is answered in general terms and clichés. Up to the present moment, the most explicit writer on this subject has been John Rewald, who surmises that Monet came here on the advice or even at the invitation of the landscape painter Charles Daubigny, and that he was drawn by a landscape 'that often shows itself in a great variety of greys, the kind of nuances to which Boudin had been so sensi-tive.'[10] I believe him to be mistaken.

4. Claude Monet, *The harbour and the Dam* (cat. no. 1).

'The Paradise in the North'

Long before the mid-nineteenth century the attractions of The Netherlands, and more specifically Holland, had made it a popular destination for Frenchmen keen on travel.[11] This appeal largely derived from the notion that the inhabitants of this wet, flat area half sunk below sea-level had created their own country, as it were, out of mud, wind, timber piles and fired clay. The singular character of the Dutch landscape with its polders, canals, dykes, channels, windmills and brick houses had always held a particular fascination for southern visitors.

In addition to this, the Northern Netherlands had shaken off the dominion of the Habsburg empire by dint of their own efforts during the Eighty Years' War (1568-1648) and for centuries since then had been a republic governed by merchants, holding its own among the powerful monarchies in Western Europe, a fact which never ceased to amaze the people of these countries. Even after Holland had itself become a monarchy in 1815, it retained an air of independence and democracy. Moreover, this little state was the nucleus of an empire stretching to the Far East, with which it had monopolised trade and cultural relations until well into the nineteenth century. Also, the Dutch, apart from their stubbornness and love of money, had a few other curious characteristics such as domesticity, cleanliness and a passion for the minute, which constantly struck foreign visitors. And finally, Holland had produced a school of painters, the non-academic nature of which was always intriguing to the French, and to others besides. All in all this sufficed to produce an almost constant stream of northbound tourists, as well as an extensive range of travel literature which began with a statement made by the Duke of Rohan in 1600: 'Holland is a wonder.'[12]

French interest in the Low Countries, then, was a long-established fact. However, in about the mid-nineteenth century this traditional appreciation developed, in certain circles, into a degree of admiration which is now hard to imagine. From the beginning of the nineteenth

18

century Dutch society was characterised by an almost complete suspension of any economic or social growth. Already distinguished by its various unusual features, the character of Holland now came to stand out more and more from that of the countries surrounding it. Here was a land which the Industrial Revolution had passed by and which seemed, also in other respects, hardly to have been touched by the spirit of the new century. The tow-boat, the traditional means of transport in these parts, became the symbol of the Dutch sense of time.

Whereas France, Belgium and Germany were rapidly being overlaid by an intricate railway system, for many years the only railway track crossing the Dutch border was the line connecting Cologne to Arnhem and Amsterdam. Until the construction of the Moerdijk bridge, in 1872, which made it possible to link north and south directly by train, the Dutch Iron Railway Company did not run to anything more ambitious than a narrow little branch line between Amsterdam and Rotterdam via Haarlem, laughingly dubbed the 'steam omnibus'. So if one was travelling by train from Paris, it was necessary to get out at Antwerp or at Willemstad on the Hollands Diep, where the railway came to an abrupt end, and to take the boat to Rotterdam via Dordrecht.[13] However, such pains were amply rewarded, for this boat transported the traveller to another world, a strange, exotic, fairy-like country: 'It is the most remarkable, the most enchanting and the most far-away country that one may pass through without leaving Europe', wrote Maxime de Camp in 1859.[14] This dream-land of peace and tranquility evoked in the minds of many travellers images of distant oriental parts, as if the age-old connection with these regions had made Holland a little bit Chinese or Japanese itself. For example, Théophile Gautier wrote in his *Caprices et zigzags* of 1865: 'With their love of porcelain, lacquer and varnish, with their scrupulous cleanliness, their dogged adherence to ancient tradition, their love of flowers, paintings and trinkets, the Dutch are immensely akin to the people of the Celestial Empire.'[15] In the eyes of a poet such as Charles Baudelaire, Holland was even endowed with the characteristics of paradise: 'There is nothing but order and beauty, abundance, peace, sensual delight.'[16]

It was not only dreamers and poets who idealised Holland, but also politically-committed intellectuals. In the minds of educated nineteenth-century men the land itself and the art and history of the country were all inextricably interwoven. Writers with republican leanings such as Théophile Thoré admired the Dutch resistance to the Spanish dictatorship under Philip II and idealised the bourgeois, 'democratic' nature of the Dutch masters.[17] As opposed to the classical Italian and French painters, who worked within the sphere of influence of court culture, these artists, after all, had chosen everyday life as their subject-matter. The philosopher Hippolyte Taine even perceived a direct relationship between this realism *avant la lettre* and the Dutch people's daily struggle against the water, which left even artists no room for exalted and speculative profundities.[18] All these French artists and intellectuals, as well as ordinary curious tourists, sooner or later felt the need to see this unique country with their own eyes. Meanwhile, keeping pace with the increasing tourism was a growing supply of travel literature, 'one of the fashions of our time', as one of the travellers remarked.[19] In their impressions and comments many of these wandering literati dwell on the landscape and the atmosphere of town and country. Their reactions are usually fully determined by the image which the old masters created of Holland. For example, Edmond Texier feels 'really, right in the middle of a painting by Aart van der Neer' during the boat journey from Antwerp to Dordrecht in 1850.[20] Other writers recognize Jan van de Velde's landscapes in the polders between Rotterdam and The Hague; Albert Cuyp on the Merwede by Dordrecht, Metsu at the vegetable market in Amsterdam or Ruisdael by an old oak in Kennemerland. It is remarkable how enthusiastically these travellers observed the art in the museums as well as the towns and the landscape around them. 'I know of no country in Europe which offers as much diversity as Holland, for all its seeming monotony', writes Texier; 'at every step the earth, the water and the buildings present elegant scenes, ready-made paintings.'[21]

5. Jan Bulthuis, *Zaandam, view from the Achterzaan*, 1794. Zaandam, Municipal Archives Zaanstad.

Windmills, Museums, Flowers and Old Gables

As regards travel guides aimed at a more general public it seems that Holland had three main pillars of attraction: firstly the impressive feats of engineering manifest in the bridges, dykes and canals, secondly the museums, and thirdly the towns, with their brick architecture so bizarre to French eyes. Amid the sundry other items singled out for attention, a few stand out as appearing in practically every guide: the windmill landscapes near Dordrecht and Rotterdam, the bulb-fields and the multi-coloured villages of Broek in Waterland and Zaandam.

After what has already been said, it comes as no surprise that all these dykes and windmills should have been objects of interest, and the same applies to the picturesque old towns. The fame of Zaandam (fig.5) dates back to the seventeenth century, when it emerged as the centre of an extensive industrial area spread over the countryside on both sides of the River Zaan, a polder-land dotted about with hundreds of shipyards, mills producing oil, corn-flour, paint, paper, tobacco and mustard, and even more than all these, saw-mills, all of which

added up to quite unparalleled landscape. The little hut in which Tsar Peter had worked for a few days in 1697 as a ship's carpenter made the village into a world famous Mecca for romantic monarchists. Moreover, Zaandam consisted largely of wooden houses built in a colourful style reminiscent of a childlike fantasy world, surpassing everything else which Holland had to offer in terms of extraordinary architecture. This led Denis Diderot, visiting Zaandam as early as 1774, to describe it as the very model of picturesque charm, more than a match for 'the romanesque compositions of the landscape painters.'[22]

During the nineteenth century, however, the glory of the village, or rather town, which status it had acquired under Napoleon, faded somewhat, and the taste of foreign visitors, too, underwent a change. Educated travellers of the mid-nineteenth century did not know what to make of the charms of the village, which they actually deemed vulgar, so that their descriptions have a curious ambivalence about them. For instance, the very thorough and serious writer A.J. du Pays opens the description in his *Itinéraire descriptif, historique et artistique de la*

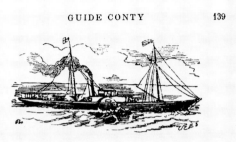

EXCURSION A ZAANDAM

Note. — Vous ne pouvez venir à Amsterdam sans visiter *Zaandam*, village célèbre où l'on voit la cabane de
Pierre le Grand, et Broek, village d'une originalité fa-
buleuse et d'une propreté exagérée.

Mais ces deux villages n'ayant aucun intérêt en dehors
de ces curiosités, nous conseillons aux voyageurs de faire
ces deux excursions dans la même journée et suivant le
programme ci-dessous.

Renseignements. — On peut se rendre d'Amsterdam à
Zaandam soit par le chemin de fer soit par le bateau. Le
mieux, selon nous, est d'y aller par le bateau et de revenir par le chemin de fer, ce qui vous permet de voir le
pays sous deux aspects différents.

Division du temps. — Matin. — *Partir le matin par le bateau, vers 8 h.; arrivée à Zaandam à
8 h. 40; visiter la cabane de Pierre le Grand, et, vers
11 h. 40, prendre le train qui vous ramène à Amsterdam; déjeuner à Amsterdam. —* Après-midi. —
*Vers 2 h., partir en bateau pour Broek (descendre à
la station de* Schouw*), et de là se rendre, en treks-
chuite ou à pied (45 minutes), à Broek; visiter Broek
et revenir à Schouw pour prendre le bateau qui passe
vers 4 h. ou 5 h. 45 du soir; dîner à Amsterdam.*

6. From: *Guide Conty: La Hollande circulaire, guide pratique*, Paris 1884.

Hollande with the firm pronouncements: 'The
excursion to Broek and Zaandam is of old a
compulsory journey for all tourists coming to
Holland. And yet, nothing is in fact less interesting and more childish than what one sees
there.'[23] Anyone who leaves Amsterdam early
and returns immediately after breakfast will be
back soon enough to do something worthwhile
with his day, is his verdict. But having said this,
our guide cannot help dwelling for pages on end
upon the countless number of windmills and
the 'houses painted green and yellow, present-
ing a most amusing appearance.' Zaandam remained, whether one liked it or not, a tourist attraction of the first order (fig. 6).

Unlike what we might expect, this was far
less the case, during this period, for Amsterdam. This city had the reputation of being a
busy, thriving commercial town, built on a

grand scale but with little of the picturesque
about it, a city with beautiful museums but no
atmosphere, although an exception was made
here for the harbours along the IJ. In 1859 Alphonse Esquiros noted that he saw few foreigners walking for the sake of walking and looking
about them.[24] The Hague was thought prettier,
Rotterdam more cheerful and sociable. This
was not only the opinion of the writers of the
guides, but also of an art-lover such as Eugène
Fromentin, who summarised his judgment in
his *Les maitres d'autrefois* of 1876 thus: 'The
colours here are strong and sombre, the shapes
symmetrical, the facades so well preserved as to
look new, with no architecture and no art, the
little trees on the waterside are spindly eyesores,
the canals are muddy.'[25] Nevertheless, there
were also French writers much earlier who
thought otherwise. The above-mentioned Edmond Texier, for instance, wrote in 1857: 'Amsterdam does not have a rich supply of monu-
ments, and yet its canals and streets offer ready-
made paintings at every step, each one awaiting
only a painter and a frame.'[26] After 1860 the
town became more and more popular, as appears from the growing production of picture
postcards, tourist maps and souvenir albums
(fig. 7). This changing appreciation for the city
has been best expressed by Emile Montégut,
who wrote exultantly in 1869 of 'the originality
of the city scene, the majestic elegance and deep
perspective of the canals, the capricious architecture of the houses and the wistful beauty of
the sunsets.[27]

Already by the time of Monet's first stay in
Holland it was considered an absolute must for
foreign travellers to view the bulb-fields. Since
the seventeenth century Haarlem had been
renowned as the international centre of the
trade in tulips, hyacinths and other exotic
bulbs. In the nineteenth century, however, ex-
ports soared to such heights that the area planted was expanded from Haarlem to the vicinity
of Leyden. This was the origin of what we now
know as the 'bulb district'. From the middle of
the century onwards, trips to the flowering
bulb-fields also became popular, and it was especially the tulip-fields that established the fame
of the region, with their wild and bizarre colour

7. *View of the Groenburgwal,* by Pieter Oosterhuis, c. 1865. Stereoscopic view: Amsterdam, Municipal Archives.

8. *The Bulbfields.* Coloured postcard: Haarlem, Municipal Archives.

combinations. Even the otherwise dry Baedeker waxed somewhat lyrical at the sight of the broad expanse of fields which 'display their varicoloured beauties' at the end of April and the beginning of May. Other guides spoke of 'famous plantations', 'magnificent gardens' or even of 'those rich lands with tulips and hyacinths, spread out over the wide fields (...) like an Indian or Cashmere shawl (fig. 8).[28]

Land of the Old Masters

Hunderds of French artists belonging to different generations and the most diverse schools, from the early nineteenth-century painters Eugène Isabey and Camille Corot (fig. 10) to the Realist Gustave Courbet and the Impressionist Eduard Manet, toured Holland during the half-century between 1840 and 1890. Thanks to work published by J. Verbeek and Hans Kraan we have approximate dates for the visits of some of these artists and know what places they went to see. Yet the nature of their journeys remains somewhat obscure, as so few of them related anything of their motives and experiences.[29]

9. Edouard Manet, *Riverscape*. Philadelphia, Philadelphia Museum of Art, W.P. Wilstach Collection.

10. Camille Jean Baptiste Corot, *Dutch landscape*. Cambridge, Syndics of the Fitzwilliam Museum.

11. Félix Ziem, *Banks of the Amstel*. Bordeaux, Musée des Beaux-Arts.

The artists' reasons for coming here will have varied just as greatly as their artistic views, but it is undoubtedly true that many of them wished primarily to enhance their knowledge of the art produced in the Golden Age. This is obvious after taking one look at the impressive list of French artists' names in the visitors' books at the Trippenhuis, which housed the Rijksmuseum collection until 1885, and at the Frans Hals Museum in Haarlem.

And outside the museums? History painters sought authentic scenery for subjects from Dutch history which were popular at the time, such as a famous sea battle, a Protestant service or an anecdote from the Eighty Years' War. Others felt the need to study the Dutch masters in their own environment, and to measure themselves against them, in the conviction that these masters 'had done nothing other than to paint what they saw.'[30] We know, for example, that Corot and Troyon alternately visited museums and sketched out-of-doors with equal zeal.[31] Manet, too, who certainly came to Hol-

land mainly for the museums, did some painting outdoors; witness his audacious Dutch River-view in the Philadelphia Museum of Art (fig. 9). Dutch landscapes were apparently much loved by the French public, as the sales catalogues of the art-dealer Durand-Ruel, among others, make clear.[32] They were also shown frequently in the Salons, the official Paris art exhibitions, and the state purchased a Dutch landscape on more than one occasion. The catalogue of the *oeuvre* of the Romantic painter Félix Ziem lists no fewer than six versions of the same sunset with tall windmills on the Amstel (figs. 11, 12)![33] Jongkind also returned to Dutch themes dozens of times in order to satisfy the demands of the Paris public (fig. 14).

The artists' itinerary, in common with that of the art lovers, was fairly uniform: it kept more or less to the route Dordrecht - Rotterdam - The Hague - Haarlem - Amsterdam. These were the best-known Dutch towns, they were connected by the railway line, and the larger museums and private collections were also to be

24

12. Félix Ziem, *Holland*. Baltimore, The Walters Art Gallery.

found here. In addition, this route was thought to embrace the areas depicted by the old masters: the windmills of Dordrecht and Rotterdam, the polder-lands of South Holland, the Scheveningen beaches, The Hague Wood, the dunes near Haarlem and the River Amstel by Amsterdam. And even those artist whose interest in the themes of the old masters was less pronounced adhered to the tradition in not venturing beyond this area.

Monet and the Colour of Zaandam

Why, then, did Monet not follow this tradition? All the enthusiastic stories of the Dutch museums and the picturesque landscape must certainly have reached him. But it is questionable whether Monet was actually interested in having the same experiences. Almost apologetically he writes to Pissarro from Zaandam that he has not yet had time to visit the museums, because he has to paint first. Not until weeks af-

ter his arrival did he go to the Rijksmuseum, after having met two other art lovers. At the Frans Hals Museum, where Courbet, face to face with the Haarlem master, had had the experience of his life, Monet signed the visitors' book no earlier than October, when he was already, as it were, on his way home to Paris. The immense shock so many of his contemporaries felt at the confrontation between the art of the past and the reality of the present was for Monet, it seems, no longer an issue.

He was not the only one. There were other fellow-artists, some of whom were older than he was, who adopted a freer attitude towards the Dutch old masters, building on the innovations of the Barbizon School. This is true, in the first place, of Johan Barthold Jongkind, the Dutch Frenchman who, with his emphasis on painting in the open air, was the precursor of the Impressionists (fig. 13). He and Monet had been friends since their first meeting in 1862, and Monet regarded Jongkind, who was 21

25

13. Johan Bartold Jongkind, *The main gate at Rotterdam.* Private collection.

14. Johan Bartold Jongkind, Title-page of *Cahier de Six Eaux fortes, vues de Hollande.* The Hague, Municipal Museum.

years older, as his true master. Jongkind certainly must have recommended that Monet acquire first-hand knowledge of the peculiar Dutch light, as he may have inspired two other artists to visit Holland during those same years, although later than Monet: Eugène Boudin and Charles Daubigny (fig. 15). At first sight this relationship seems an adequate explanation for Monet's journey to Holland and his stay here. The suggestion gains more weight when we compare Daubigny's Dutch landscapes with some of Monet's Zaandam paintings, one of which Daubigny later bought (cat. no. 11). However, it is a curious fact that whereas Boudin and Daubigny, just as Jongkind himself, immediately set off for the area of Dordrecht and Rotterdam, Monet did not spend a single day there but took the first train to a town which none of his predecessors had thought worthy of a canvas. The majority of Monet's

26

15. Charles Daubigny, *Mills in Holland*. Lisbon, Calouste Gulbenkian Museum.

Zaandam and Amsterdam paintings are also completely different in terms of atmosphere and colour from those of his pre-Impressionist friends from the Channel coast.

Monet's sudden journey and his long stay in Zaandam become more intelligible, in my opinion, if we note that in those very years he was searching for a landscape art in which it was no longer the delicate tonality that held sway, but intense, primary vigour and the authenticity of unmixed colours. That he should have sought inspiration in Holland for such purposes sounds surprising; after all, we are used to seeing Holland as the land of grey, subdued shades. It was primarily the painters of the Hague School who, encouraged by the example of the Barbizon School, represented the effects of damp and haziness on the colours of the land with a palette in which often the slightest trace of colourfulness was suppressed (fig. 17). There was nothing more splendid to Jacob Maris, for instance, than 'a dingy day.'[34] The great popularity of the 'Grey School' for generations determined our appreciation of the Dutch landscape.

There were also many French authors in the mid-nineteenth century who emphasised,

16. Eugène Boudin, *Dutch Mills*, 1884. Douai, Musée de la Chartreuse.

with approval or otherwise, the greyness of Holland. Arsène Houssaye, an influential art critic and one of Monet's first buyers, composed a sonnet to 'this grey landscape' in 1844.[35] Louis Vitet saw 'the entire country beneath a dreary, misty sky, opaque and without colour.'[36] Taine sat from ten until three o'clock on the IJ, one September day in 1858, watching how 'the sea changes colour every half-hour, now the colour of pale lees, then a chalky white, then again yellowish like wet mortar, or black-

17. Johan Hendrik Weissenbruch, *Sunset at Boskoop*. Private collection.

ish like diluted ink. The clouds look exactly like the round and ripped apart masses of steam from a locomotive; the whole is grand, strange, sick.'[37]

But this was not how everyone saw it. Especially somewhat younger authors were struck precisely by the extremes in the weather and landscape. On this subject Emile Montégut wrote: 'The mobile and extremely changeable appearance of Holland has two aspects: it is radiant, it is melancholy.'[38] Henry Havard, of whom more will be said in due course, actually fulminates in his *Histoire de la peinture hollandaise* against the supposition that 'the Dutch climate must above all be gloomy, murky, black and misty'. If so, the light in the paintings of the Dutch masters must surely have been invented in their studios, Havard continues rhetorically. No, of course not, for Holland, where the damp ensures that the polders are always a constant green, may well be the most colourful landscape in the whole of Central Europe: 'The sky above and the water in which the sky is reflected beneath are both silvery-white or of an extremely pale azure; between the sky and the earth are the houses with their red roofs and brown walls and the big, black windmills with their gaudy sails the colour of ochre or saffron. Altogether these go to make up a total palette of unprecedented vividness; brown against white, red against green, orange against blue; can anything be dreamt of that is more full of contrast, warmer, more powerful?'[39]

It is tempting to see a connection between on the one hand, the changing appreciation for the various features of the Dutch landscape in the nineteenth century, and on the other hand, the history of the art of painting during the same period. The generation of Houssaye, Vitet and Taine had grown up with the art of Corot and the Barbizon masters. They shared with them not only a love of the 'realistic' Dutch school, but also a taste for sober landscapes whose value was determined by the wealth of tonal variations in the light. That the 'naturalness' of this art of landscape painting was only relative, was keenly felt by an occasional observer belonging to the same generation. Théophile Gautier notted in 1865, after a journey by diligence through northern France on his way from Paris to the Low Countries: 'The sky was superbly, thickly painted, with a broad, bold stroke; as regards

28

the land, I thought it far less successful; the lines were cold, the colours dry and glaring; I do not understand how nature could look so unlike anything natural and so closely resemble ugly dining-room wall-paper. (...) the real scenery seemed to me to have been painted, and then actually no more than a clumsy imitation of the landscapes of Cabat or Ruisdael. This idea came into my mind more than once while I was looking out of the window at those endless strips of chocolate-coloured earth gliding by, together with rows of trees of the most delectable spinach-green that one can imagine. Any artist who ventured to depict such foliage and such fields would doubtless be accused on all sides of not having painted naturally; it all looked as if it had been punched out by a machine, with inconceivable crudity, harshness and a lack of any atmospheric perspective; the murals in a gymnasium, on which one sees large lawns reminiscent of the cloth on a billiard-table, alleys in *café au lait* and houses that seem to be sporting [yellow] nankeen trousers come closer to nature than one would think.'[40]

It is clear that Gautier had no liking for those aspects of nature which the Impressionists actually sought out, although it may well have been the very confrontation with their work which taught him to look at the landscape the way he did.

Concerning the Dutch landscape as seen by Havard, colourful and rich in contrasts, we have already seen that Zaandam possessed these qualities to an almost exaggerated degree, so much so that an educated man of Gautier's generation would have been expected to turn his nose up at it. But some of the younger writers did not do so; in any case, Maxime du Camp, poet, art critic and Levant traveller, did not. In his *En Hollande; lettres à un ami*, published in 1859, he writes effusively of Zaandam, unrestrained by the aesthetic preferences of his time. He has never seen so many windmills in his life, it is a 'whirling of blades in all corners of the horizon'. Du Camp is also struck by the 'amusing imaginativeness' of the architecture: 'It is lively, genial and very highly-coloured. The bowsprits of the boats nudge the quay, where there are rows of wooden houses painted green, grey and

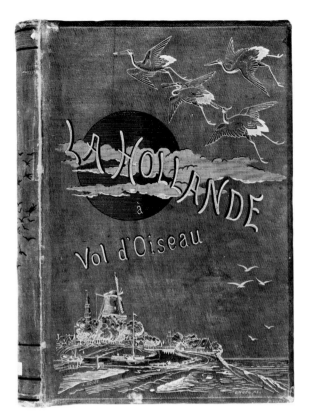

18. Cover of Henry Havard, *La Hollande à vol d'oiseau*, Paris 1881.

pink, set off with bright hues, surprisingly cheerful and a feast for the eyes, which have tired of the omnipresent even red colour of Dutch brick.'[41]

It all reminds one strongly of Monet writing to Pissarro of the 'houses of every colour, hundreds of windmills and enchanting boats, (...) the most delightful things everywhere'. It also puts one in mind of the colourful contrasts, not to say downright showiness of some of the Zaandam canvasses, which differ so greatly from the grey paintings Monet produced in London, but to which some of the French paintings from the preceding period had provided the first impulse.[42] After his letters to Pissarro no other statements made by Monet have been preserved as to what it was about the character of the Zaandam landscape that particularly attracted him. There is, however, an indirect source: the writings of his travelling companion Henry Havard.

19. Maxime Lalanne, *A Zaandam (Hollande)*, 1877. From: Henry Havard, *La Hollande à vol d'oiseau*, Paris 1881.

An art-loving merchant

Havard was a merchant with an artistic sense and republican leanings, who had been forced to flee from his country because of his share in the Commune of Paris, shortly before Monet met him in Zaandam. How he ended up in Zaandam we do not know, but we do know that from this first visit onwards, he developed into an art-historian and became the author of a whole series of books about Holland and Dutch art (fig. 18). As a memento of the weeks they had spent together in Hotel de Beurs, Monet gave him a little painting with a view of Zaandam (cat. no. 19). Together with a third guest, the painter Henri Michel-Lévy, they visited the Trippenhuis, strolled through Zaandam and went rowing on the Zaan.

This visit evidently made a deep and lasting impression on Havard. In *Amsterdam et Venise*, published in 1876, he describes the arrival by boat: 'Straight ahead of us we see the pretty village cheerfully spread out amid a mass of foliage. The houses are black or grey, yellow or green, with bizarre shapes and odd decorations. (…) The church with its pointed steeple, the town hall and that inn with a balcony that has such an oriental look about it [Hotel De Beurs!, B.B.] admirably complete this extraordinary tableau. All those small houses scattered haphazardly on both sides of the lock, which proudly bears the arms of the town and those of the province, all those boats with their brown hulls, their red sails and their little flags make up the strangest harmony of shrill and false notes. Brick-red, chrome-yellow, black and spinach-green clash with each other, resulting in the most unusual composition of sharp tones that one could wish for. But all this is softened, tempered and as if melted by the luminous atmosphere in which all is bathed and which succeeds in fusing all these crude colours into a whole that only pleases, and is a treat to behold.'[43] Parts of this passage could serve to describe works which Monet painted at Zaandam Harbour. It is as if we were reading a literary form of the comments the young merchant jotted down from the artist's lips.

30

20. Vincent van Gogh, *Flower beds in Holland*. Washington, National Gallery, Collection Mr. and Mrs. Paul Mellon.

But Zaandam, 'The China of Holland', as Havard terms it, had more to offer than out-landish buildings in ostentatious colours.[44] Beyond the Dam and between the gardens of Oostzijde and Westzijde flowed the Zaan, a liv-ing illustration of that other, elegiac Holland which had caused so many visitors to lose them-selves in thoughts of distant lands (fig. 19). As far back as 1775, for Father Francois-Xavier de Feller, Zaandam had evoked the image of Chi-na, on account of the low houses of painted wood and the shaded waters.[45] Du Camp too had admired the Zaan, as it lay there, broad, gently rippling, surrounded by green gardens and colourful tea-houses which reminded him of Constantinople. Henry Havard calls the Zaan 'the loveliest river one could hope to find. Wide, calm and full to the brim it flows between two banks covered with trees and flowers, among which nestle a multitude of houses, belvederes,

kiosks constructed of wood and painted in the most diverse and the strangest of colours. The tall trees and absurd houses are mirrored in the river, which also reflects the blue sky with its big white clouds. Picture this to yourself for a moment and you will fancy yourself instantly transported to China, Japan, perhaps the In-dies.'[46] After reading the above, no-one will be left feeling surprised that Monet painted the Achterzaan in the elegiac mood desscribed here, with the 'Chinese' tea-houses (cat. no. 6).

The painter and the writer must have walked about together not only in Zaandam, but also in Amsterdam. The following is a pas-sage taken from the written record Havard kept of his walks through the city. Having arrived on the left bank of the Inner Amstel he continues: 'The Groenburgwal opens out before us, domi-nated in the background by the magnificent tower of the Zuiderkerk. Here again is a charming and complete painting, the kind that is scarcely forgotten once it has been seen, causing one to wonder in surprise why it has not been reproduced by painters more often.'[47] Then follows a lengthy description of the 'painting', for the time a very unusual, colourful description, which gives the reader as in other sections the feeling that he is being allowed to look over Monet's shoulder with Havard at the canvas that is on the easel (cat. no. 34). Havard, in fact, is enchanted by Amsterdam, a city 'that takes on colour with a force, an intensity that almost defies belief.' And again we are reminded of Monet, this time of the almost impudent gaudiness of some of his Amsterdam canvasses (cat. nos. 33, 35).

It seems very likely that Havard's enthusiasm as to this particular aspect of the Dutch landscape was greatly influenced by his association with Monet, the more so if we consider that the educated public of the years around 1870, excepting an occasional individual such as Maxime du Camp, decidedly did not share this preference. However, Havard too was later uneasy, as indeed was Gautier, who was much older, concerning the colour effects which the Impressionists conveyed on their canvasses. This is clear from his first notice of an Impressionist exhibition, dating from 1879, in which he writes of Monet and Pissarro: 'I humbly confess that I do not see nature as they do; these pink cotton-wool skies, this water of opaque moiré, this multi-coloured foliage I have never seen. They may exist. I do not know them.'[48]

Monet, Art and Tourism

Let us return once more to the question posed at the beginning: why did Monet come to Holland? It has already been noted that, certainly until about his fortieth birthday, he was something of a stay-at-home painter. The remark made in his first letter written from Holland, to Pissarro, immediately upon arrival 'What I saw of it seemed far more beautiful than it is said to be' makes one suspect that Monet had not been so very convinced of the beauties of this country. One may wish to doubt whether the artist

21. George Hitchcock, *Hyacints in Holland*. Whereabouts unknown.

undertook this journey solely on his own initiative, or whether he may have met people in London who directly inspired him to do so; the French art-dealer Durand-Ruel, for instance, to whom Monet had been introduced by Daubigny and who, according to his bookkeeping records, bought two landscapes from the painter in June 1871, that is to say, just after Monet had left for Zaandam.[49]

Regarding Monet's visit to the bulb-fields in 1886, we know for certain that Durand-Ruel acted as a mediator. Just as fifteen years earlier in Zaandam and Amsterdam, there was a motif highly attractive to tourists, but as yet hardly discovered by painters. With his rendering of the bulb-fields, surprisingly colourful for his Hague period, Vincent van Gogh was one of the exceptions (fig. 20). Apart from him we can only name the fairly obscure Haarlem painter Anthonie Lodewijk Koster and the American-

22. Anthonie Lodewijk Koster, *Flower beds in Holland*. The Hague, Municipal Museum.

born George Hitchcock, who lived in Holland, as having produced a number of views of flowering bulb-fields from the late 1880s onwards (fig. 21,22); Ferdinand Hart Nibbrig also tried his hands at this motif some years later.

That Monet was not averse to such tourist motifs is indeed common knowledge. It was travel guides and tourist leaflets which provided the impetus for his visit to the picturesque Côte d'Azur, a region so favoured by the general public. Did the same also apply in the case of Holland?

We have already seen that Monet returned at least once to Amsterdam, and perhaps also to the Zaan. Had he grown so attached to the two places that pure art induced him to pay one or two more undocumented fleeting visits to this country? Or were there also other reasons? It has been mentioned above that Amsterdam had become very popular with tourists by about 1870. In this context it should also be noted that nearly all of the Amsterdam canvasses show

exactly the same spots as were available on a large scale during this period in the form of engravings, lithographs, cabinet photographs and stereoscopic photographs in Amsterdam as well as in Paris (fig. 23). Among the most popular views painted by Monet are the Groenburgwal with the Zuiderkerk, the Inner Amstel with the Munt tower, the windmill on the Onbekende Gracht and the Oude Schans with the Montelbaans tower (cat. nos. 33,34,30,28). Monet even produced two almost identical versions of the view of the Groenburgwal (as of the view of the corner houses on the Kromme Waal) (cat. nos. 33,34). One of these (cat. no. 33) was purchased in Paris in 1906 by the grandfather of the present owner, not because he was so fond of Monet, for the artist was unknown to him, but because he had so enjoyed himself during a holiday trip in Amsterdam that he was eager to possess a colour souvenir of the city (the other painting he acquired on this occasion was a nude).[50]

23. *Souvenir d'Amsterdam*, Haarlem (1875).

We should not forget that until the rise of the Expressionists and non-representational art, that is to say well past the turn of the century, such a motive for buying a work of art was not looked upon as in any way peculiar or barbaric. Only the real connoisseur bought a painting exclusively for the quality of the *peinture*. And for an artist, before the twentieth century, there was not the slightest disgrace in repeating a painting with a theme that sold well, more than once if need be, certainly not if the artist in question was always as short of cash as Jongkind or Claude Monet. A good art-dealer mediated between artist and customer, which implied that he had a sharp eye for the kind of landscape motifs or areas which would both interest 'his' painters in an artistic sense and appeal to the future buyer in their subject-matter. All in all, there are a sufficient number of indications to suspect that economic considerations, alongside purely artistic motives, were of greater than marginal importance for Monet's visits to Holland, and especially the one to Amsterdam. It may also have played a role that Zaandam was known as a millionaire's village owing to the lucrative industrial windmills and that Amsterdam was still considered one of the richest cities of Western Europe.

If Monet and Durand-Ruel had ever hoped to do business with one of these affluent Dutchmen, they must have been disappointed. Aside from one or two portraits, Monet did not sell one painting to a Dutchman. In Holland the public was even more reluctant than in Paris to be open towards the quality of his pictorial experiments. The following comments on the second Impressionist exhibition, written by the young writer Marcellus Emants, who was thought of as belonging to the avant-garde in Holland, constitute a typical case in point: 'As regards the landscapes, I do not believe that the worst decorations of the grimiest theatre, anywhere in the world, have anything to show which could compete with the nauseating herring-salads being dished up here. Mr. Monet paints ships scarlet and sky-blue with bright yellow masts, bluish-green trees, yellow houses and chrome-coloured duck-weed on ultramarine water. Presumably he had just purchased new paints when he was seized by the idea of throwing a few splotches of the most glaring colours onto a canvas, and of painting a lady in the midst of it, supposedly taking a morning turn in the garden. Much good may it do her eyes!'[51]

* Much of the content of this article goes back to discussions with Willem van Bennekom, with Ronald de Leeuw and with my fellow-authors Arend Huussen, Joop Joosten, Ronald Pickvance and Ernst van de Wetering. Marijke de Groot provided assistance in collecting the literature, as a part of a training programme at the Municipal Archives in Amsterdam. Finally, I am extremely grateful to Louis van Tilborgh for his critical support. Bev Jackson translated the article from the Dutch.

1. See Appendix II, 3.
2. The biographical aspects and in particular the political background to Monet's first visit are dealt with in the contribution by A.H. Huussen, following on the present one.
3. See Appendix II, 4.
4. See Appendix III, 7.
5. Daniel Wildenstein, *Claude Monet: Biographie et catalogue raisonné*, 4 vols., Lausanne & Paris 1974-85, vol. 1, letter no. 60.
6. *De Portefeuille* 8 (1886-87), 8-5-1886.
7. See Appendix II, 5.
8. Duc de Trévise, 'Le Pèlerinage de Giverny', *Revue de l'art ancien et moderne*, 1927, pp. 126-127. Most Dutch tulips are cultivated for the bulb, which grows every season, thanks to the nourishment drawn from the plant. To concentrate growth in the bulb, the plants are 'topped' and the flowers removed in vast quantities, before reaching the stage at which they will wilt.
9. See Appendix II, 6.
10. John Rewald, *The History of Impressionism*, New York 1973, p. 263.
11. See R. Murris, *La Hollande et les Hollandais au XVIIe et au XVIIIe siècles, vus par les Français*, Paris 1925; Madeline M.C. Koumans, *La Hollande et les Hollandais au XIXe siècle, vus par les Français*, Maastricht 1930; and H. van der Tuin, *Voyageurs français au Pays-*

Bas dans la première moitié du XIXe siècle, Lille 1935-36.

12. Henri duc de Rohan, *Voyage faict en l'an 1600, en Italie, Allemagne, Pays-Bas uni, Angleterre et Ecosse,* Amsterdam 1646, p. 2.

13. A concise overview of the problems with the railways after about 1850 can be found in L.G.J. Verberne, *Geschiedenis van Nederland in de jaren 1850-1925,* 2 vols., Utrecht 1957, (originally published as *Geschiedenis van Nederland,* ed. H. Brugmans, vol. VIII, Amsterdam 1938) vol. 2, p. 84 ff.

14. Maxime du Camp, *En Hollande, lettres à un ami, suivies des catalogues des musées de Rotterdam, La Haye et Amsterdam,* Paris 1868, p. 249; the first edition dates from 1859.

15. Théophile Gautier, *Caprices et zigzags,* Paris 1884, p. 89; the first edition appeared in 1865.

16. Charles Baudelaire, 'L'invitation au voyage', *Les fleurs du mal,* ed. Yves-Gérard le Dantec, Paris 1941, p. 57.

17. W. Bürger (ps. Théophile Thoré), *Musées de la Hollande,* 2 vols., Paris 1858-1860, vol. 1, pp. IX-XI, vol. 2, p. XIV.

18. H. Taine, *Philosophie de l'art dans les Pays-Bas: Leçons professées à l'Ecole des beaux-arts,* Paris 1869, p. 30.

19. Emile Montégut, *Les Pays-Bas, impressions de voyage et de l'art,* Paris 1869, p. 1.

20. Edmond Texier, *Voyage pittoresque en Hollande et en Belgique,* Paris 1857, p. 4.

21. Ibid.

22. Denis Diderot, *Voyage de Hollande,* published in 1774; in: *Oeuvres complètes,* 5 vols. and supplement, Paris 1819, suppl., p. 74.

23. A.J. du Pays, *Itinéraire déscriptif, historique et artistique de la Hollande,* Paris 1862, p. 263.

24. Alphonse Esquiros, *La Néerlande et la vie hollandaise,* Paris 1859, p. 80.

25. Eugène Fromentin, *Les maîtres d'autrefois,* Paris 1883, p. 314; the first edition dates from 1876.

26. Texier, op. cit. (note 20), p. 164.

27. Montégut, op. cit. (note 19), p. 299.

28. K. Baedeker, *Belgique et Hollande, manuel du voyageur,* Coblenz 1866, p. 252; *Guide Conty; La Hollande circulaire, guide pratique,* Paris 1884, p. 108; Du Pays, op. cit. (note 23), p. 180; Esquiros, op. cit. (note 24), pp. 5-6.

29. J. Verbeek, 'Bezoekers van het Rijksmuseum in het Trippenhuis, 1844-1885', *Gedenkboek uitgegeven ter gelegenheid van het honderdvijftigjarig bestaan van het Rijksmuseum,* The Hague 1958 (special issue of the *Bulletin van het Rijksmuseum* 6 (1958)), pp. 60-71; Hans Kraan, 'Holland in zwang', in exhib. cat. *The Hague School; Dutch Masters of the 19th century,* London (Royal Academy of Arts) 1983, p. 124; id., 'Nederland en Barbizon, kunstenaars gaan en komen', in exhib. cat. *De School van Barbizon,* The Hague (Haags Gemeentemuseum) 1985, pp. 89-104.

30. See, for example, Montégut, op. cit. (note 19), p. 106: 'Backhuyzen, who, like all his Dutch compatriots, did nothing other than to faithfully reproduce what he saw.'

31. Kraan, op. cit. 1985 (note 29), pp. 97-99.

32. I am grateful to Ronald de Leeuw for providing me with this piece of information.

33. Pierre Miquel, *Félix Ziem, 1821-1911,* Maurs-la-Jolie 1978, vol. 2, e.g. cat. nos. 1549 and 1593.

34. The term was introduced by J. van Santen Kolff, as were the names 'Hague School' and 'Grey School', both used by him in *De Banier* of 1875. See Gerard Brom, *Schilderkunst en literatuur in de 19e eeuw,* Utrecht 1959, p. 96.

35. Arsène Houssaye, 'Philosophie du voyage', in *Voyages humoristique; Amsterdam, Paris, Venise,* Paris 1856, p. 90 (appeared previously in *De Kunstkronijk* 1844-45, p. 31).

36. See Henry Havard, *Histoire de la peinture hollandaise,* no place of publication given, 1881, p. 12.

37. Letter from Taine to his mother, d.d. 7 Sep. 1858, in: *H. Taine, sa vie et sa correspondance,* vol. 2, Paris 1904, pp. 168-69.

38. Montégut, op. cit. (note 19), p. 147.

39. Havard, op. cit. (note 36), pp. 11-14.

40. Gautier, op. cit. (note 15), pp. 6-7.

41. Du Camp, op. cit. (note 14), pp. 165-66.

42. See Appendix II, 4.

43. Henry Havard, *Amsterdam et Venise,* Paris 1876, pp. 257-58.

44. Ibid., p. 268.

45. François-Xavier de Feller, *Itinéraire, ou Voyages de Mr. l'Abbé de Feller en diverse parties de l'Europe...,* Paris & Liège 1823, p. 251.

46. Havard, op. cit. (note 43), p. 238.

47. Havard, op. cit. (note 43), p. 263.

48. Henry Havard, *Le Siècle,* 27 April 1879; quoted in exhib. cat. *The New Painting: Impressionism 1874-1886,* Washington (National Gallery of Art) 1986, p. 180, cat. no. 81.

49. John House, 'New Material on Monet and Pissarro in London in 1870-71', *The Burlington Magazine* 120 (1978), p. 640.

50. This information by kind courtesy of Comte d'Arschot, who conveyed it to E. van de Wetering.

51. Marcellus Emants, 'De salon des refusés te Parijs', *Nederlandsche Kunstbode* 3 (1876), p. 75; I am grateful to Louis van Tilborgh for providing me with this quotation.

CLAUDE MONET IN HOLLAND

A.H. Huussen jr.

Whatever the exact occasion may have been for Monet's journey to England in the autumn of 1870, there is every reason to view his visit against the background of the situation in his own country at the time. This was the precise period during which diplomatic developments between France and Prussia came to a head. A conflict had arisen regarding the succession to the Spanish throne. The Spaniards themselves expressed their preference for Prince Leopold of Hohenzollern, who was married to one of the daughters of the King of Portugal. Twice he went as far as to decline to ascend the throne, but renewed pressure applied by, among others, the Prussian Chancellor Otto von Bismarck, caused him to yield. However, for reasons of security the French government were not willing to tolerate the presence of a German monarch at their southern border. After a diplomatic incident the French authorities eventually took the decision to mobilise, on 15 July 1870, and four days later an official declaration of war reached Berlin.

Within a few weeks the two countries were enmeshed in a long-expected war. Six weeks later matters appeared to have been decided by Heinrich Karl von Moltke's superior Prussian strategy and France's failing military leadership. On 2 September 1870 Marshal Macmahon was forced to surrender with no fewer than 82,000 men – some sources even give 106,000 – at Sedan in north-eastern France. Emperor Napoleon III, who had been taken a prisoner-of-war, abdicated and left for England, but in Paris a republican 'National Defence' government moved into power on 4 September. Meanwhile German troops were advancing on the capital; by 18 September they had sur-

rounded the city and laid siege to it. On 29 January 1871 a peace treaty was signed at Versailles. Eleven days earlier, on 18 January, the King of Prussia had been proclaimed Emperor of a federate state of Germany in the Hall of Mirrors at the Palace of Versailles.

Monet's visit to England

On 9 September 1870, a few days after the proclamation of the republic, Claude Monet was in Le Havre, far from Paris. It is not entirely clear whether, similarly to others somewhat later, he was indeed driven from the vicinity of Paris by the advance of the German troops, as has been occasionally suggested. In any case it is apparent from a letter the artist wrote that day to his friend, the landscape painter Eugène Boudin, that he suffered from an acute lack of funds.[1] He was obliged to ask his friend to pass on a letter he enclosed to Camille, who was still in Trouville. Monet describes the predicament of hundreds of travellers hoping to seek refuge in London who were left stranded on the quays of Le Havre. As will become apparent, Monet himself had secured a passport. This would seem to indicate that he was also intending to cross the Channel. He may have entertained the idea of first following Boudin to Morlaix on the northern coast of Brittany. In any case his presence is documented in London at the end of November 1870. There he met Charles Daubigny, who introduced him to Durand-Ruel, a dealer with plans to open an art gallery in New Bond Street. Thus an artistic and business relationship was forged which was to become immensely important for Monet, and for the impressionist painters in general. Monet exhibited in London in

December 1870 and March 1871.[2]

At the end of May 1871 Monet wrote to his friend Camille Pissarro, with whom he had had frequent contact in London, that he was intending to leave.[3] Two documents make it clear that Monet arrived in Zaandam no later than 2 June 1871. A one-line note with this date requests the French committee of International Exhibition in London to release two seascapes with their frames.[4] The extensive letter he addressed to Pissarro from the Hotel de Beurs in Zaandam on the same day is much more informative: 'We have finally arrived at the end of our journey, after a rather unpleasant crossing. We traversed almost the whole of Holland, and, to be sure, what I saw of it seemed far more beautiful than it is said to be. Zaandam is particularly remarkable and there is enough to paint here for a lifetime: I believe we are going to be very well housed here. The Dutch seem most friendly and hospitable.'[5] Monet inquires of his friend after the situation in Paris. From the moment of leaving London they had been quite without any news, and French newpapers were unobtainable in Zaandam.

Why did Monet, Camille and their son Jean leave London for Holland? Surely there were things to be done in France after so long an absence. And what led them to the unlikely destination of Zaandam, apparently from Rotterdam? The first of these questions may possibly be answered on the basis of indications in Monet's letters to Pissarro. In that of 27 May, mentioned above, we find a slightly enigmatic passage: 'You have undoubtedly heard of the death of poor Courbet, shot without trial. The vile conduct of Versailles. It is all too atrocious and sickening. I cannot put my heart into anything. It is all utterly distressing.'[6]

It is quite plausible that Monet, maybe urged by his Dutch friend, the landscape painter Johan Barthold Jongkind, sought inspiration in the Dutch water-landscape. However, it seems more likely that the political situation in France, and more especially in Paris, disrupted his plans: his return was not yet opportune. In order to grasp the background features not only of Monet's visit but also those underlying the concern of the Dutch authorities regarding his stay, some remarks are in order at this point on the continued unrest in Paris, with the people's dismay at the capitulation of their new republican government.

The Commune of Paris

Shortly after signing the treaty of Versailles the radicals, supported by armed members of the national guard, established their own government in the Paris city hall. They called themselves the 'Commune' in commemoration of similar events that had taken place during the Revolution of 1792-93. The aim was a radical socialist policy which would drastically reform the social structure of Paris in the direction of a democracy, and this meant civil war. The French government, which had its seat in Versailles, took over the siege of Paris from the Germans, who kept at a distance.

One of the Commune's sympathisers was the painter Gustave Courbet, who had been one of the witnesses at Monet's wedding on 28 June 1870. The artist played a modest part in the cultural policy of the Commune. He was appointed as president of the 'Société des peintres' and on 12 April 1871 the executive committee charged him with the reopening of the Paris museums to the public and with the organisation of an annual exhibition of paintings. This official function and his alleged role in the destruction of the Vendôme Column led to his arrest in June, after the Commune had been overthrown. On 2 September he was sentenced to six months imprisonment.[7]

It is clear, then, that Monet was mistaken in believing that his friend Courbet had been executed, as he wrote in his letter to Pissarro on 27 May. But such a misconception was understandable. For in the week of May 21-28 French government troops retook the capital, violently suppressing the Commune with a great deal of bloodshed. A wave of retaliation followed.[8] In a word, the situation in Paris was grim indeed. There was reason enough for Monet not to have wished to return at that stage. He had apparently seen enough of London for the moment, so decided to visit Holland.

Yet Monet was not simply a tourist in Holland. He was a Frenchman arriving at the precise moment of time at which the Commune was being crushed. There was little appreciation here for the radical-socialist experiment. On the contrary, in Holland, as elsewhere in Europe, the general public and the authorities viewed it with repugnance. This can easily be gleaned from the critical comments on the events in Paris appearing weekly in the *Zaandamsche Courant*. On 22 April 1871 this liberal newspaper, published by G. Dekker Cz., likened the leadership of the 'red of republican party' to a lunatic asylum run by *furiosi*. On 3 June it informed its readers that the Commune had been defeated. Whilst its columns dubbed the participants brutish beasts, comparable to bloodthirsty tigers, restraint was advocated in the prosecution and trial of the Communards.[9] People greatly feared the machinations of the Socialist International who were – wrongly – suspected of being the driving force behind the Commune uprising.[10] In Holland the Commune was adduced as the reason for shelving a bill, introduced into Parliament on 30 April, which was to have lifted the ban on coalition government.[11] Not only in the Dutch Parliament, but also in the daily press, the Commune was cast in the villain's role; the events of May 1871 coincided with the Dutch election campaign.[12]

There was yet another respect in which the government was involved in the vexed question of the Commune, for the French Minister of Foreign Affairs, Jules Favre, had submitted formal requests, dated 26 May and 6 June 1871, for the extradition of Communards who had fled the country.[13] So the Dutch authorities were faced with the awkward problem of deciding what to do in the unhoped-for event of these very persons seeking refuge in Holland. The embassies in London and Berne apprised the Dutch government of the attitudes of the English and Swiss governments respectively. The English were inclined to regard the Communards as criminals whereas the Swiss preferred to look upon them as political refugees. In the former instance there was a clear-cut case for expelling the fugitives as undesirable aliens; given the latter stand, the granting of political

asylum could be considered. Apparently the Dutch authorities adopted the same position as the English. [14]

French visitors in Holland

According to an interesting file in the Dutch Department of Justice, police and customs officers were very much on the alert for Frenchmen entering the country.[15] On 4 June 1871 Aloys Breton, a bank clerk from Paris, was discovered in the border town of Arnhem. Being a Communard he was put over the border at Roosendaal on 11 or 12 June. On 31 May the Chief Commissioner of Police in the seaport of Rotterdam had inquired of his colleagues in Belgium, where a number of Frenchmen must surely have taken refuge, whether they also intended to resort to deportation. On 7 June officials of the 'sureté publique' in Brussels wrote in response that in three cases only, travel papers for Holland had been issued to persons believed to have participated in the Commune. These were Thomas Javorski, Paul Kunachowicz and Henri André Aguillon. The first two men had Commune passports, the third a 'legitimate' one.

The Chief Commissioner of Police in Rotterdam thought it wise to pass on the information received to the Minister of Justice, the more so as a rumour was circulating that Victor Hugo planned to journey from Brussels to Holland. Also, the Chief Commissioner requested to be given some guidelines for procedure with respect to foreigners of this category who entered the country:

'When it was rumoured that *Victor Hugo* was removing from Brussels to Holland in order to settle either in Amsterdam or here, I considered it my duty to make the following request to the Chief Commissioner of the sureté publique in Brussels. I urged him to inform me in good time, should it be the case that Frenchmen regarded as constituting a menace to the peace, whether members of the Commune or supporters of its association, having been expelled from Belgium, were enabled to proceed by way of the Grand

Central Belgian Railway to Holland. In answer to this application I received the enclosed missive, of which I respectfully submit a copy to your Excellency, with kind request to inform me as to the procedure to be followed in connection with those mentioned above or similar persons, should they desire to settle here or to pass through.'[16]

The Minister of Justice followed hierarchical procedures by giving instructions to the Attorney-General of the province of South Holland without delay. His letter of 9 June reveals that he was of the opinion that each case should be treated on its own merit, in the light of the Aliens Act and the extradition treaty with France:

'In the enclosed letter the Chief Commissioner of Rotterdam asks to be advised as to the procedure to be followed with regard to aliens connected with the affairs of the Commune who should chance to appear in these regions. It would appear to me that this matter can only be resolved by referring to the Aliens Act and the extradition treaty with France. Each case which presents itself will require separate consideration and must be dealt with in accordance with the provisions of the said law and the said treaty. However, the Chief Commissioner will be well advised, should any alien of the category concerned appear in Rotterdam, to consult your Honour with respect to the measures to be taken in the case at hand. Your Honour will then be able to determine whether it is appropriate that the sentiments of the government be inquired after.'

It was not only the Rotterdam Chief Commissioner who was so vigilant. As the Commissioner of Police in Zaandam was alarmed at the arrival of an alien originating from France, the Attorney General of the Amsterdam courts of justice also went into action. On 8 June he sent a telegram to the Minister of Justice containing the following piece of information (fig. 24):

'According to a telegram received from the Police Department in Rotterdam, Victor Hugo is intending to journey to Amsterdam. The Commissioner of Police at Zaandam has apprised me of the arrival there of one Claude Monet, 31 years of age, a painter, born in Paris, accompanied by his wife and child. He has travelled from London and intends to take up residence in Zaandam for some time practising his art. He is in the possession of a passport issued under the Empire on September 5th 1870 [added in pencil: 'Day of proclamation of the Republic]. Although he is not a suspect person at the present time I am having his movements closely observed.'

Here again Victor Hugo has a role in the proceedings. The renowed French writer had been elected as a representative in the republican National Assembly before the emergence of the Commune. But he had soon resigned in disappointment, and sought voluntary exile in Belgium. He had taken no part in the Commune, but after he had publicly criticized the Belgian extradition policy concerning fugitive Communards, the government expelled him on 30 May. This accounts for the apprehension that Hugo might be coming to Holland. As it was, the rumour turned out to be false, for Hugo made his way to Vianden in Luxemburg.[17]

Obviously it is the information relating to Claude Monet that is of particular interest for our purposes. The Attorney-General did not consider him a suspicious person, for his passport dated from the period of the Empire – though only just! Moreover, he had come from London. Nevertheless, the police in Zaandam watched his movements closely: one could never be sure! The Zaandam Police Commissioner had informed Schooneveld about Monet on 2 June 1871:

'Notification is given of the arrival in this city of an alien, one Claude Monet, 31 years of age, a painter, born in Paris. He

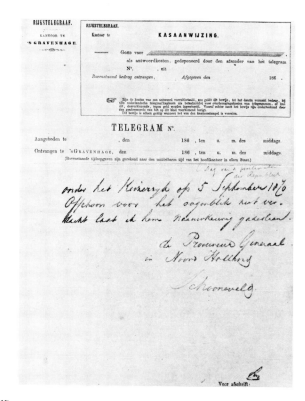

24. *Telegram*, dated 8 june 1871. The Hague, Public Record Office.

is presently lodged at the Hotel de Beurs, proprietor Mr. Kellij. Mr Monet's passport was issued under the Empire and is dated September 5th 1870. He is accompanied by his wife and child, and intends to take up residence here for some time to practise his art. He has travelled from London. Although I have observed nothing in connection with the said alien to arouse suspicion, it appeared to me to be an appropriate discharge of my duty to apprise your Honour of this circumstance, which duty I respectfully fulfill herewith.'[18]

Initially the Commissioner reported conscientiously on Monet's comings and goings in his weekly reports to his superior officer in Amsterdam. On 5 June he had 'nothing to report' with regard to the foreigners. Two weeks later, on 19 June, he states that 'to date Claude Monet has done nothing to invite suspicion.' On 22 June he sent another letter concerning the arrival of two new guests:

'At the Hotel de Beurs in this town, proprietor Mr. Kellij, two aliens have arrived with the intention of remaining at the said address for some time to come. Their names are Henry Havard, a merchant, born at Charolles (Soane et Loire), resident in Paris, aged 33, and Henrij Michel Levij, a painter, born and resident in Paris, aged 27. Both are in the possession of foreign passports, the first being dated May 27th 1871, issued by the Préfect du Nord at Lille for Belgium and Holland, the second dated June 1871 and issued by the French legation in Brussels.

On 26 June the Commissioner reassuringly wrote in his week report: 'The movements of the Frenchmen previously mentioned as residing here, to wit Monet, Havard and Levij, do not yield anything remarkable. They seek each other's company a great deal, and go for walks or at times row on the Zaan. The two painters are seen working from time to time.' A month later, on 31 July, he reported that Michel-Lévy

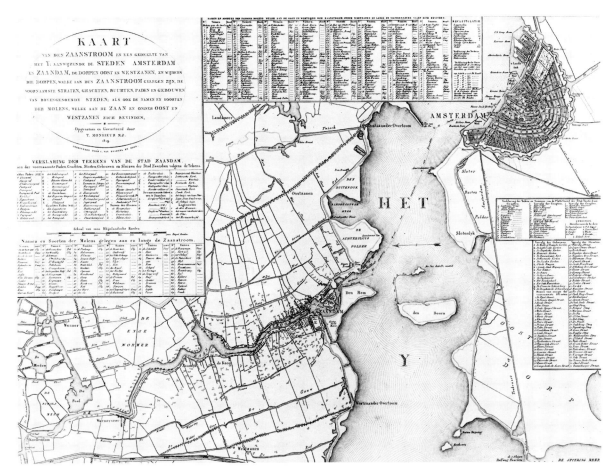

25. T. Monsieur, *Map of the Zaan (...) and Amsterdam*, 1819. Amsterdam, Municipal Archives.

had returned to France; Monet was the only one left. So Havard had evidently gone too. On 9 October the Zaandam police official was able to notify his superior (with perhaps a note of relief?): 'On 8 October the Frenchman Claude Monet, accompanied by his wife and child, left by boat for Amsterdam to continue their journey from there within a few days' (fig. 25).

The authorities in Zaandam had one thing less to worry about. Thanks to their vigilance and to the fact that they were obliged to provide weekly reports, and thanks also to the resourceful research of the Zaandam regional historian J.D. Bakker, we know that Monet headed for Paris, by way of Amsterdam, no earlier than 8 October. It was apparently on his return journey that Monet visited the Frans Hals Museum in Haarlem as Michel-Lévy had done before him (fig. 27).[19]

We do not know whether Monet was aware of the keen interest in his activities on the part of the Dutch authorities. It seems likely that the Zaandam police would have informed him of the special attention he commanded when Monet reported to show them his passport and register the required personal data. He seems to have remained unconcerned about it, and rightly so. Indeed in his letter to Pissarro dated 17 June 1871, he remarks: 'I have just met Lévy, the other painter who is obliged to spend some time here. I have not yet had time to visit the museums. What I want first of all is to work, and I will allow myself all that later.'[20] This break in his work schedule soon came. From the visitors' book at the *Trippenhuis* in Amsterdam we know that Monet went to see the collection there on 22 June 1871, in the company of Havard and Michel-Lévy (figs. 26, 28, 29).[21]

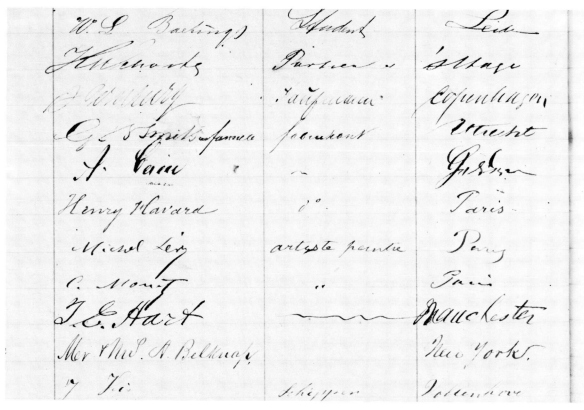

26. Signatures Henry Havard, Henri Michel-Lévy and Claude Monet. Visitor's book of the Trippenhuis. Amsterdam, Rijksmuseum Printroom.

Monet in Holland

Aside from the above-mentioned documentary evidence we know virtually nothing about Monet's stay in Zaandam. Tradition has it that his wife, Camille, gave French conversation lessons there. We know with certainty that Monet was acquainted with one particular Zaandam family at least, the Van de Stadts, an established family of merchants and manufacturers: Monet painted the portrait of the 16-year-old Guurtje (cat. no. 25).[22] According to a family tradition Monet is also said to have produced a portrait of Willem Boot (1831-1899), captain of the Zaandam paddle-steamer 'Prins Willem van Oranje'. Monet supposedly kept up regular contact with the Boot family.[23]

As we know from one of the weekly reports issued by the Zaandam police, Monet and his family left Zaandam on 8 October to return home

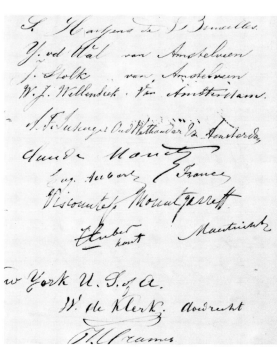

27. Signature Claude Monet. Visitor's book of the Frans Halsmuseum. Haarlem, Municipal Archives.

ζὺν ὅλῃ τῇ ψυχῇ .....!

Henri Havard

28. Emile Bertaux, *Henry Havard*. Paris, Bibliothèque Nationale.

by way of Amsterdam. With exception of a short visit to a museum there is no documentation for his stay in Amsterdam. Still, the artist and his wife sat for a portrait to the photographer A. Greiner (fig. 30, 31).

As Monet returned to France at the end of October or the beginning of November 1871, he could have worked a few weeks in Amsterdam. Oddly enough, however, two of his paintings show Amsterdam in the snow (cat. nos. 36, 37), the others seemingly stemming from a different season. On the basis of the former piece of evidence as well as the striking stylistic discrepancies between these and the Zaandam works, there has been some speculation as to the possibility that the Amsterdam scenes originate from a later visit to Holland. Although the literature on Monet usually alludes to a Dutch stay in 1872, with no further documentation, Monet's biographer, Wildenstein, believes that the Amsterdam paintings should be assigned to 1874, on biographical and stylistic grounds.

The biographical argument *e silentio* which Wildenstein advances is the complete lack of any data concerning Monet's life between 23 January and 1 April 1874. In his opinion the weather conditions in Amsterdam during this period justify the conjecture that Monet worked there at the end of the winter and at the beginning of spring.[24]

As to his first visit to Holland, we definitely know that he was back in his Paris studio in the Rue d'Isley near St. Lazare Station by 19 November 1871. It appears from the other letters to Pissarro in 1872 and 1873 that Monet spent most of the time at Argenteuil.[25] On 2 January 1872 his good friend Eugène Boudin informed M. Martin that 'We often meet Monet; we dined in fine spirits in his new home at Argenteuil a few days past. He has a splendid house and appears to relish the notion of establishing a certain position for himself. He has brought back some very beautiful studies from Holland and I think he is destined for the highest ranks of our movement.'[26] In fact, the studies were not all that the artist had brought home from Holland. In some of the paintings of his Argenteuil garden, huge stone pots are seen with designs in blue – Cologne pots, I would say – which Monet, as tradition has it, had transported home from his Dutch journey in 1871 (fig. 32). We find the same pots adorning a later painting, produced in 1880, of his garden at Vétheuil.[27]

Monet paid a final visit to Holland in 1886. His circumstances had changed considerably in the intervening fifteen years. It was Baron d'Estournelles de Constant, the embassy-secretary to the French legation in The Hague, who invited him to Holland, as is clear from a letter of Monet to his friend Théodore Duret (fig. 33). The 1886 visit was once again documented on the part of Holland. However, this time it was not the police authorities who followed him. His presence was the occasion for a few remarks in the periodical *De Portefeuille* in the issue of 8 May 1886: 'The well-known French painter Claude Monet, one of the most talented of the impressionists and renowned in Paris, has come to this country, where he has previously sojourned and worked more than once before, to

29. Edgard Degas, *Henri Michel-Lévy*. Lisbon, Calouste Gulbenkian Museum.

30. *Oscar Claude Monet*, by A. Greiner, Amsterdam 1871. Photo: Private Collection.

31. *Camille Monet-Doncieux*, by A. Greiner, Amsterdam 1871. Photo: Private Collection.

produce impressionist studies of tulip-fields. The brightly varied tints of these flowers, as brilliant as Persian rugs, will undoubtedly hold out a great deal of attraction to this painter.'[28]
In the meantime, the character of Monet's travels had changed sharply. To the extent that we have been able to fathom the artist's motives, it was the war situation in September 1870 that caused the initial travel to London. A combination of political factors and the advice of friends probably decided him not to return to France in the spring of 1871, but to wait until peace was restored after the Commune uprising in Paris. However, the charms of Zaandam and Amsterdam kept him enthralled for an unexpectedly long time.

1. Daniel Wildenstein, *Claude Monet: Biographie et catalogue raisonné*, 4 vols., Lausanne & Paris 1974-1985, vol. 1, p. 427.
2. For Monet's visit to London, see J. House, 'New material on Monet and Pissarro in London in 1870-71', *Burlington Magazine* 120 (1978), pp. 636-42; pages 678-81 contain his review of volume 1 of Wildenstein's biography.
3. See Appendix II, 1.
4. See Appendix II, 2.
5. See Appendix II, 3.
6. See Appendix II, 1.
7. On Courbet, see R. Fernier, *La vie et l'oeuvre de Gustave Courbet: Catalogue raisonné*, 2 vols., Lausanne & Paris 1977-78, and exhib. cat. *Gustave Courbet (1819-1877)*, Paris (Musée du Grand Palais) 1977.
8. See for instance J. Bruhat (ed.) et al., *La Commune de 1871*, Paris 1970, exhib. cat. *La Commune de Paris dans le livre et l'image*, Brussels (Koninklijke Bibliotheek Albert I) 1971. There is a contemporary 'historical study' of these events by the socialist F. Domela Nieuwenhuis: *De Fransche burgeroorlog van het jaar 1871*, Haarlem [1881].
9. See the comments in the foreign affairs columns of the *Zaanlandsche Courant*, housed in the Municipal Archives at Zaandam. I am grateful to Titia de Groot of the

Zaanstad Municipal Archives for her assistance in making copies available of this and other sources.

10. J.J. Giele, *De eerste Internationale in Nederland: Een onderzoek naar het ontstaan van de Nederlandsche arbeidersbeweging van 1868 tot 1876*, Nijmegen 1973, pp. 108, 111-12, 116, 120-21, 125-26. See also *Zaanlandsche Courant* 12 August 1871, p. 2, and 19 August 1871, for the article entitled 'De Internationale'.

11. A.H. Huussen jr., 'Coalitieverbod en stakingsvrijheid. Sociaal-rechtshistorische aspecten van de wet van 12 april 1872 (Stb. 24)', *Economisch- en Sociaal-historisch Jaarboek* 45 (1982), pp. 96-113; esp. 100.

12. A. Doedens, '"Stad van bloed en gruwelfeesten... 't Hemeltergend wuft Parijs." Nederland en de Commune-opstand van 1871', *De Negentiende Eeuw* 9 (1985), pp. 193-206.

13. Bruhat, op. cit. (note 8), chapter 9; Domela Nieuwenhuis, op. cit. (note 8), p. 114.

14. On the enforcement of the Aliens Act of 1849 and that of 1875, see J.B. Gorsira, *Toelating en uitzetting van vreemdelingen*, The Hague 1894.

15. General State Archives, The Hague, material compiled by H. Bonder, *Archieven van het departement van Justitie 1813-1876*, The Hague 1933, p. 69, no. 5201, 'Weren van gevluchte Parijsche opstandelingen. 1871'. All references and quotations derive from this title.

16. For this letter of 8 June, see previous note. I have previously directed attention to these documents in 'Claude Monet in Zaandam en Amsterdam in 1871', *Jaarboek van het Genootschap Amstelodamum* 66 (1974), pp. 156-64 and 'Claude Monet aux Pays-Bas', *Septentrion* 5 (1976), pp. 85-95.

17. Exhib. cat. *La Commune de Paris...*, op. cit. (note 8), nos. 243-44: Victor Hugo, *Carnets intimes 1870-1871*, ed. H. Guillemin, Paris 1953, pp. 138-42; Ph. van Tieghem, *Dictionnaire de Victor Hugo*, Paris 1970, p. 37 and M. Granet, *L'évolution de la pensée politique et sociale de Victor Hugo d'après son oeuvre postérieure à 1848*, Paris 1973, pp. 456-66 and 486-90.

18. Copies of this letter as well as the weekly reports quoted on the following pages all derive from the Zaanstad Municipal Archives; see Appendix III, 1-7. I am especially grateful to J.D. Bakker, for tracing these copies and making them available. In the archives of the Attorney-General, housed in the State Archives in Haarlem, no correspondence has been handed down from 1871; information by courtesy of the State Archivist.

19. For the signature, of around 10 October, see Haarlem Municipal Archives, Archives of the Frans Hals Museum, no. 102 (visitors' book 1862-1872); Michel-Lévy's visit was at the beginning of June.

20. See Appendix II, 4.

21. J. Verbeek, 'Bezoekers van het Rijksmuseum in het Trippenhuis 1844-1885', in: *1808-1958 Het Rijksmuseum: Gedenkboek ter gelegenheid van het honderd-*

vijftigjarig bestaan, The Hague 1958 (special issue of the *Bulletin van het Rijksmuseum* 6 1958), pp. 64-65. On foreign artists visiting Holland, see H. Kraan, 'Franse schilders en Nederland', in: exhib. cat. *De school van Barbizon: Franse meesters van de 19e eeuw*, The Hague (Haags Gemeentemuseum) 1985, pp. 97-104, and id., *Als Holland Mode war: Deutsche Künstler und Holland im 19. Jahrhundert*, Bonn 1985; and Petra ten Doesschate Chu, *French realism and the dutch masters*, Utrecht 1974. The visitors' book for the Amsterdam Fodor collection only goes up to 1860: Iris Hagenbeek-Fey, 'Carel Joseph Fodor (Amsterdam 1801-1860) en zijn schilderijenverzameling', *Antiek* 10 (1975), p. 27.

22. Guurtje Van de Stadt was the eighth of ten children born to Jan Van de Stadt and Alida Mats. She was born on 2 October 1854; on 11 July 1878 she married Ericus Gerhardus Duyvis. She died on 5 January 1936. Her youngest daughter Guda Duyvis, born in 1894, married the well-known Professor of prehistory from Groningen, A.E. Van Giffen; see *Engel van de Stadt 1746-1819, zijn voor- en nageslacht*, The Hague 1951, pp. 195 and 197-200.

23. Information by courtesy of the Schoen and Boot families, in connection with an article by P. Kok on Monet in *De Typhoon: Dagblad voor de Zaanstreek* 2 April 1975, p. 7. Some time ago, F. Mars carried out some important research on Monet's stay in Zaandam, of a historical-topographical nature. See Mars' articles 'Zaans schoon', *De Zaende* 3 (1948), pp. 112-21; 'De Franse schilder Claude Monet in Zaandam', ibid., 4 (1949), pp. 378-82; 'Claude Monet' in: M.A. Verkade et al., *Zaandam 150 jaar stad 1811-1961: Bijdragen tot de ontwikkelingsgeschiedenis van de stad*, Zaandam 1962, pp. 323-35; 'Een franse schilder in Zaandam (1870-1871)', *Noord-Holland: Tijdschrift gewijd aan de situatie in Noord-Holland* 11 (1966), pp. 165-75; and an untitled typescript (Zaandam, 1967), in the 'G(emeente) Z(aandam) Heemkunde' series, to be found in the Zaandam Municipal Archives.

24. Wildenstein, op. cit. (note 1), vol. 1, pp. 70-71.

25. For the letters, see Wildenstein, op. cit. (note 1), vol.1, p. 428.

26. G. Jean-Aubry, *La vie et l'oeuvre d'après les lettres et les documents inédits d'Eugène Boudin*, Neuchatel 1968, p. 82.

27. Exhib. cat. Paris 1980, pp. 227-29, cat. no. 83 and pp. 151-53, cat. no. 52; Wildenstein op. cit. (note 1), vol. 1, p. 61, cat. nos. 202, 284, 685 and 365. For general remarks on this subject, see P.H. Tucker, *Monet at Argenteuil*, New Haven & London 1982.

28. *De Portefeuille* 8 (1886-87), 8 May 1886, note by courtesy of J. Joosten.

* The article was translated from the Dutch by Bev Jackson.

32. Claude Monet, *The Garden*. Whereabouts unknown.

33. Letter of Claude Monet to Théodore Duret, dated 3 May 1886. Paris, Archives Durand-Ruel.

DUTCH REALITY AND MONET'S ARTISTIC 'DECEIT'*

Ernst van de Wetering

Monet's traces in Holland are still fresh. His movements through Zaandam, Amsterdam and the bulb-region can be followed virtually everywhere. Discovering the spot where he must have stood with his easel strongly evokes the feeling which Johan Huizinga called 'the historical sensation': a sudden realization that the past has really existed and that it can, so to speak, be touched. However, the consequent excitement is accompanied by a certain dismay: on the spot where he stood amidst the bulb-fields, a motorway has been built; the garden in Zaandam where he painted the houses opposite, has forever vanished under a factory, and the Amsterdam harbour is not what it used to be either. But the paintings turn back the clock for a while. They seem to prove that, a century ago, these places really looked the way Monet's paintings evoke them. Yet there are reasons to ponder on the relationship between reality and art in the case of Monet's Dutch paintings and to examine the particular problems that must have occurred when these works were created.

Plein-air painting

One of the painters with whom Monet several times painted from nature, Pierre Auguste Renoir, used to say: 'When painting outdoors, one is always deceiving.'[1] It is intriguing to retrace to what extent Renoir's statement applies to Monet as well. In fact, another of Monet's friends, Paul Cézanne, once said: 'Monet is only an eye, but – good God – what an eye!', suggesting that Monet was a living camera objectively capturing what he saw.[2] So could it be that Renoir's statement on deceiving when painting outdoors did not apply to Monet?

The classical anecdote illustrating how impossible it is for a painter to render an objective picture of reality, can be found in the autobiography of an older contemporary of Monet's, the German painter and illustrator Ludwig Richter. Richter remembered how he and a group of artist friends once sat drawing the same landscape in Italy. It was the period in which such topographic views were captured with a sharp pencil and the greatest precision. Having finished, Richter and his friends were surprised to see that their renderings of the very same motif differed much more than they could have imagined.[3] None of them will have had the feeling that he had been deceiving – to use Renoir's words. But because of this experience, the inevitable fact that everyone sees reality in his own way dawned on Richter and his friends.

Monet must have experienced the very same sensation when he sat painting the same motifs at La Grenouillère together with Renoir, their easels side by side (figs. 34, 35). Could it have been the striking differences between their final results which prompted Renoir to make his statement?[4]

It is a sufficiently well-known fact that plein-air painting was a matter of principle for Monet. In the case of a large figure-piece portraying women in a garden, for instance, he even went so far as to dig a trench in his garden in order to sink the painting partly into it, so that he could reach the upper part of the enormous canvas; only to be able to continue working outdoors consistently, in front of the motif.[5] Painting from nature did have some tradition, by then, but it had been the custom to use the paintings sketched outdoors as material for 'real' paintings to be produced in the studio.[6]

34. Pierre Auguste Renoir, *La Grenouillère*, 1869. Stockholm, National Museum.

35. Claude Monet, *La Grenouillère*, 1869. New York, Metropolitan Museum of Art.

36. Pierre Auguste Renoir, *Monet painting in his garden in Argenteuil,* 1873. Hartford, U.S.A., Wadsworth Atheneum, bequest of Anne Parrisch Titznell.

Monet was one of the first to believe that the definitive, finished painting also had to be created outdoors. Later he said: 'I threw myself body and soul into plein-air painting. It was a dangerous innovation. No one had done it before.'[7]

There are two rather nice testimonies from Monet's Zaandam period proving that he painted outdoors in Holland as well. There is the report written by the superintendent of police in Zaandam stating that, apart from taking walks and rowing on the Zaan, he was seen plying his trade from time to time.[8] The other testimony has been handed down by word of mouth in a farming family near Zaandam: Monet is said to

have asked their great-great-grandfather's permission to paint in his meadow.[9]

We can picture the way Monet stood painting there by looking at an 1873 painting by the same Renoir who saddled us with the problem of 'deceit' in plein-air painting (fig. 36). In his right hand, Monet holds a brush at the far end with a relaxed gesture, his eyes focused on his motif. Later photographs prove that Renoir had captured Monet's painting gesture truthfully (fig. 37). Underneath the easel is a painter's box and also a folded white sun-shade which was to protect the painter from being blinded by the sun.

37. *Monet painting in his studio in Giverny in 1913.* Photo: Archives Wildenstein.

38. Claude Monet, *The Mill 'Het Oosterkattegat'* (cat. no. 21).

39. Detail of fig. 38.

40. Detail of fig. 38. The relief - and partly the colour - of an outpainted large ship is visible on the right of the green reed.

Monet, however, was not only a fair-weather painter. An 1868 newspaper article gives a vivid description of how he stood painting outdoors, knee-deep in the snow, and there are many more stories – by others, but also by Monet himself – how he kept defying the weather time and again.[10] Only the rain, understandably, tied him to the house; the Dutch weather, therefore, will often have been too much for him. How he tried to solve this problem is illustrated by two Zaandam paintings. One of these is a rapid sketch in oil, perhaps executed between two showers of rain (fig. 42). The other one is a painting executed on the canvas format he regularly used for his Zaandam works, depicting the same subject once more (fig. 43).[11] It is a rather void, obviously unfinished painting. On the grounds of the strong similarity between these two works, it can hardly be doubted that Monet painted the larger version – indoors, in his hotel room – from the sketch. He never signed these two canvases. They remained unsold, and bear the signature stamp wich was put on the works found in his studio after his death.

Several more instances are on record of

41. Claude Monet, *The Voorzaan and the IJ* (cat. no. 24).

canvases that were executed in the studio, based on sketches painted outdoors. It is evident, however, that Monet, as a rule, considered these canvases to be his 'stepchildren'.[12] Not until his later years, when he painted the monumental Water Lilies series, did he work from sketches, for obvious practical reasons.

Stage props

When comparing the afore-mentioned paintings, an interesting difference is noticeable: the two sailing ships on the left-hand side of the sketch have been moved to the right-hand side of the larger painting (figs. 42, 43). Evidently, Monet was not satisfied with the role of the ships in the first composition. The correct position of the elements was obviously of importance to Monet's 'objective eye'. More instances can be found of such alterations in the composition of his Zaandam paintings. Hidden underneath the layer of paint of *The Mill 'Het Ooster-kattegat'* (fig. 38), in the space between the bank and the large, dark vessel ploughing the open waters (fig. 39), is a ship of nearly the same size with a red sail which was painted over by Monet at a later stage (fig. 40). The suggestion of the movement of the ship was emphasized by widening the space behind the ship. Monet used

the same 'mise en toile', as he called it, in another painting (fig. 41). The ship with the white sail to the right of the dark ship has been placed more in the foreground of this painting. In both paintings he decided to use a sail, projecting above the border of reeds, to indicate that the water is widening there into the waters of the IJ (figs. 40 and 41). So, ships are being moved here like stage props. This is, of course, inevitable in the case of ships, since they are too mobile to be captured straight away. It cannot be a coincidence that the most prominent ship in the two paintings also appears in one of the drawings done in Zaandam (p. 125, fig. 19). Such manipulation of moveable elements is, of course, also done with other moveable parts of reality. Also in the case of human figures, the painter must choose which moment of their movements he is going to fixate and where he is going to situate them (unless, as Renoir once did, he takes his brother along to enter into conversation with passers-by on all sorts of pretexts, to make them stand still for at least a while).[13] In this context, it is immediately obvious that there are hardly any people in Monet's Zaandam paintings. Human figures will completely vanish in his later works, aside from the shadowy indications of townspeople in his Paris and also his Amsterdam paintings (fig.

42. Claude Monet, *The Voorzaan and the Westerhem* (cat. no. 16); oil-sketch for cat. no. 17 (fig. 43).

63). One of the recurrent human stage props in Monet's Zaandam works seems to have been his wife Camille, who appears in a number of paintings as an elegantly-dressed lady (cat. nos. 6-8, 15). Here, the painter revealed himself as a manipulator of reality, and this must, undoubtedly, have been one of the things Renoir was thinking of when he spoke about 'deceit' when painting outdoors.[14]

The artist is, of course, also free to manipulate the fixed elements in the landscape. For the benefit of his painting, he can embellish them, move them or simply leave them out. However, upon examining the topographic accuracy of Monet's paintings, it appears that he has been extremely faithful in this respect.[15] Yet, some of the Zaandam paintings give a distorted picture of reality. For the views of the Voorzaan and the Westerhem, for instance, Monet has chosen his viewpoint in such a way that the opposite bank falls just outside the picture-area (figs. 42, 43, 46), thus creating the incorrect impression that the water continues boundlessly to the right. He did the same with the views of the Zaan flowing into the IJ (figs. 38, 41). In one of his Amsterdam paintings he appears to have left out the elevated part of the drawbridge in the background (cat. no. 29). The reasons are obvious: this hoisting apparatus would otherwise have disrupted the clarity of the railing and the passers-by on the bridge in the foreground. But such interferences with the topographic reality hardly ever occur, as far as can be checked.

Viewpoint and composition

An obvious form of manipulating reality was, of course, the choice of the spot on which to paint. The British art historian John House, who made a thorough study of Monet's working-methods, has collected numerous testimonies by Monet and others which clearly show how much attention he paid to finding the right viewpoints for his compositions.[16] The fact that he often chose stereotype views of scenic places is no coincidence and does not have to be attributed to opportunism on his part. After all, popular views are often, and rightly so, praised because of their picturesqueness. The fact that they were also characteristic of a town or a country, is something which Monet was certainly interested in. In the case of one journey abroad, he wrote that the paintings he took home should give the right impression of the places he had visited.[17] This must be the main reason why the Amsterdam paintings are rather stereotype in their choice of subject, of viewpoint and, therefore, of composition.

In Zaandam, he must have felt less tied, in this respect. This is shown by Monet's first letter to Pissarro, in which he wrote that he could go on painting all his life, there.[18] In another part of this book, Boudewijn Bakker demonstrates, surprisingly, that Holland, and Zaandam in particular, reminded the French painter of an oriental – Chinese or Japanese – place. It is remarkable, in this context, that the

43. Claude Monet, *The Voorzaan and the Westerhem* (cat. no. 17).

composition of a number of Monet's Zaandam paintings seem to have been influenced by Japanese prints, and that also the colours have the freshness of these prints. In 1893, Pissarro wrote to his son, after visiting an exhibition of Japanese prints: 'Hiroshige is a marvellous Impressionist. Monet, Rodin and I are enthusiastic (...); these Japanese artists confirm my belief in our vision.'[19] This was, admittedly, written down more than twenty years after Monet's first journey to Holland, but Monet's interest in Japanese prints can be traced back to long before that.[20] Landscape-compositions such as in Monet's Zaandam paintings, in which the eye is not guided into space from plane to plane (cat. nos. 1, 6, 9, 13, 14), are unusual in Western art, but they regularly occur in Japanese prints (figs. 44, 45). Drastically cutting off shapes in the immediate foreground is another solution which the impressionists learned from Japanese prints (figs. 46, 47).

With almost all the Zaandam pictures, the place from which Monet painted them can be comparatively accurately indicated. It is, however, not always clear whether Monet was standing on land or whether he sat working on a moored ship or in a rowing-boat. We know

from his later years that he often used a boat; Edouard Manet has left us a splendid document of this (fig. 48). A considerable number of his Zaandam paintings also appear to have been executed from a boat. Perhaps Monet took this idea from Charles Daubigny, with whom he had become friends during the months in London which preceded his stay in Zaandam.[21]

A floating studio such as this must have had all sorts of advantages. In view of Monet's great interest in the way things are reflected in water, a boat offered an ideal opportunity to choose the right viewpoint. The same advantages were found at sites such as the Sluice of the Noordervaldeursloot, the Ganzenwerf, the garden of the Van de Stadt family along the Zaan, and the moored ships in the vicinity of the Dam; only two Zaandam pictures were painted in the streets: *The Blue House* and *The Footbridge* (cat. nos. 15, 19). It may of course be that Monet usually chose his motifs near the water because of a desired composition or because of his obsession with reflections in water. But a much more trivial reason should not be overlooked: they are practically all places where he was not bothered by the inevitable ring of lookers-on collecting around a painter in the street.

57

44. Claude Monet, *Mills in the Westzijderveld* (cat. no. 13).

The fleeting moment

Wherever Monet was standing or sitting, virtually all his paintings appear to be accurate, topographically. Yet even in his pursuit of topographic accuracy, Monet was constantly forced to make a choice. The reality around us is so mobile and variable that a painter can do no other than select, even if he is determined, as the impressionists were, to capture the fleeting moment as literally as possible; Monet's entire oeuvre testifies to how seriously he took this determination. Time, however, kept catching up with his endeavours, until he decided to have a separate canvas ready for each moment of the day, each change of atmosphere and light. This development came about by gradual stages. Later in life, Monet once said in an interview: 'When I began, I was like the others: I thought that two canvases were enough, one for dull weather, one for sunshine.'[22] The first two canvases that are known for certain to have been used this way, were painted in Amsterdam. They are two views of the Groenburgwal. One

is kept in subdued greys (fig. 49), the other has been painted in bright sunlight (fig. 50). We can easily picture Monet at work on a day with clouds drifting past: two canvases of the same size ready at hand, alternately on the easel.

During his Amsterdam stay he evidently went to work with two canvases on another day: this time to the Montelbaans-tower. The weather remained fair, and the artist needed only one canvas; at full speed he did a 'shorthand' painting of the townscape (fig. 51). The sea ships indicated by their masts in the background provided the subjects of his second canvas (fig. 52). The striking similarities between these two pictures – the same execution, the same size, an identical colour of the primed canvas (the pieces of canvas even come from the same bolt) – make it tempting to presume that Monet walked on for a few hundred metres from the Montelbaans-tower and set up his easel again near the harbour.[23] The incidence of light in both pictures supports such a reconstruction of a day in the life of Monet. In the painting of the Montelbaans-tower the light

45. Hokusai, *The stone bridge at New Mountain, Aji river, Osaka.* Amsterdam, Rijksmuseum Printroom.

comes from the south-east, witness the shadowed façade to the right; this was in the morning. In the view of the harbour, the light, judging from the arrangement of light and shade on the rowing-boat in the foreground, comes from the south-west; therefore, it was the afternoon.

In Amsterdam two canvases were sufficient, but Monet took more and more canvases along, in the course of time. This is illustrated by a splendid description by Guy de Maupassant, who observed Monet at work in 1885: 'Off he went, followed by children carrying his canvases, five or six canvases representing the same subject at different times of day with different light effects. He picked them up and put them down in turn to the changing weather.'[24] Still later, when he painted the numerous versions of two views of the Thames from his London hotel room, he was surrounded by more than a hundred canvases.[25]

From this point of view, a lot of 'deceit' must have been needed to capture just one moment on one canvas which he worked on for

hours, if not for days, as was the case with his Zaandam paintings. In fact, he was not always successful. The Neo-impressionist Paul Signac once remarked that two kinds of light could be seen within one painting, 'the light of two o'clock in the afternoon and of five o'clock in the evening'.[26] This happened to Monet with his *View of the Zuiddijk* (fig. 53), in which the foreground is still bathed in the afternoon light, whereas the Zaandam town hall in the background is illuminated by the evening sun from the west (fig. 54). In that painting, moreover, an earlier pale blue sky appears to have been replaced by a brighter blue sky filled with billowing white clouds. It is quite understandable that Monet sometimes grumbled about clouds which should – or should not – be present.[27] In his *View of the Voorzaan and the Island*, executed in a flash, it is as if Monet has tried to keep up with time (fig. 46). Behind the roughly sketched 'repoussoir' of the moored boats, a ship is entering the composition, to the left. To the right, in the background, a large barge is tacking, sail flapping; and at the very

59

46. Claude Monet, *The Voorzaan and the Westerhem* (cat. no. 18).

last moment – this can be seen from the way in which the wet layers of paint have overlapped – Monet added the rowing-boat entering the bustle in front of the sluices (fig. 60).

Fourteen days after his arrival in Zaandam, Monet wrote to Pissarro that he had quite a number of paintings 'under way'; this can only mean that Monet still had several paintings that were, as yet, unfinished.[28] These unfinished paintings were undoubtedly waiting for the right moment to be picked up, but the changeable weather in Holland must often have kept this favourable moment waiting for a long time. Years later, in the bulb-region, Monet was luckier. At least, he remembered with satisfaction that he had the same kind of weather for days on end. Yet, also during this visit to Holland, he must have run into problems. Owing to lack of time, he had to continue working on at least one painting at his home in Giverny (fig. 55).

To what degree Monet continued working on his paintings in his studio, far away from his motif, is not entirely clear. He himself and the members of his family have, in any case, tried to keep up the myth that he painted everything eye to eye with nature. It is hard to tell from the surface of a painting what has been added afterwards in the studio. When wet paint has been applied on to dried paint, it does not necessarily mean that this was done in the studio. Monet often returned with his canvases to the same place in order to continue working, sometimes as much as a year later. In the case of his paintings from the bulb-region, it can be said with certainty – because of his short stay in Holland at the time – that the passages which were applied on to dry paint, must have been added back home, in his studio. In the discussion on Monet's 'secret' activities in the studio, John House assigns an important role to the view of the corn-mill 'De Vlinder' in Rijnsburg (fig. 55). In fact, he discovered that Monet had kept on working afterwards, on the foreground as well as on the sky, obviously with the intention of achieving stronger colours.[29] Can a similar experience have induced Renoir to stop painting outdoors, in 1883? It had happened too often to him that a painting created out of doors lost all its power, once inside.[30] Monet may have had a similar experience when he came home from the bulb-region with his 'harvest'.

The poor palette

The most obvious problem of rendering nature is that reality has to be translated into paint. Monet was fully conscious of this problem.

47. Hiroshige, *Sunrise at the beach near Shiba*, c. 1830. Amsterdam, Rijksmuseum Printroom.

48. Edouard Manet, *Monet on his floating studio in Argenteuil in 1874*. Munich, Neue Pinakothek.

49. Claude Monet, *The Groenburgwal and the Zuiderkerk* (cat. no. 33).

When he was painting in Italy for the first time, he wrote to Théodore Duret: 'It is terribly difficult, I should have a palette with diamonds and jewels, to be able to paint this.'[31] He was overwhelmed by a similar feeling when faced with the Dutch bulb-fields, about which he wrote: 'they are quite admirable, but drive the poor artist mad, they cannot be rendered with our poor palette.'[32] The fact that he kept searching for other technical solutions should perhaps be explained from this feeling of powerlessness.

The various Dutch periods show Monet in successive stages of his search for a more and more adequate translation of reality into paint. He dit not, by the way, look for a solution in greater precision and sharpness. In fact, he avoided sharp delimitations to an ever greater extent. James Whistler, the British painter, once said to Monet that he: 'never delimited his forms, whereas nature often delimits.' Monet answered: 'Yes, doubtless nature does, but light never does.'[33] The rendering of light was Monet's most important objective, from the beginning. Later in life, Monet said that he did not depict objects, but the atmosphere and light enveloping these objects.[34]

The swift, rough touch played an important role in Monet's creation of the illusion of reality on the canvas. Though he greatly varied his brushwork, his touch always remains visi-

62

50. Claude Monet, *The Groenburgwal and the Zuiderkerk* (cat. no. 34).

ble. The visible brush stroke had been appreciated for centuries, in particular by connoisseurs. There is an interesting 17th-century book, existing only as a manuscript, containing a chapter listing phrases which connoisseurs might say to a painter to praise his work. One of the phrases recommended in it is: 'How is it possible that the brush can have given such softness by such rough touches, and that such apparent carelessness should be so attractive.'[35] Monet could, in fact, count on the roughly painted works being eagerly bought by fellow painters and real connoisseurs, while intending the more detailed, elaborate paintings for art-dealers and collectors.

The first design of his paintings was always extremely sketchy, it only provided a very global arrangement of forms, light and colour. This stage of a painting was called the 'ébauche'.[36] It is not always clear how consistently he applied this technique.[37] In the paintings from the bulb-region, this stage of the work can be recognized in many places between the touches applied afterwards. They are bright colours, thinly brushed out, which permitted the painter to leave some parts of his painting untouched. The painting of bulb-fields in the Musée Marmottan has partly remained in this state (fig. 57). It is noteworthy that the 'ébauche' is completely lacking in two of the

63

51. Claude Monet, *The Montelbaanstoren on the Oude Schans* (cat. no. 28).

three Amsterdam paintings which I have been able to examine in detail (fig. 51, 52, 58, 59). Here, a light grey priming functions as a 'safety net', on which he could work very scantily without having it become a coloured drawing; this would have happened if Monet had painted the same way on a white priming. It was only later that he would practically always use white primings, but by then his technique had become more complex: he deliberately wanted to prevent people from seeing from the surface how he executed his paintings.[38]

It is remarkable that Monet managed to put these two Amsterdam pictures directly on to the canvas without any preparation. Monet must obviously have had a fabulous command. Cézanne once said to someone who watched him painting: 'How easy it is to deform that shape. I try as hard as I can and find it terribly difficult. Monet has that great ability. He looks, and, straight away, draws it in the right proportions.'[39] Traces of rapid sketching can occasionally be recognised in the Zaandam paintings, but also in these cases he must often have painted virtually directly on the (usually yellowish) ground which functioned as a 'safety net'; there were no 'holes' when the canvas was partially left uncovered.

The great change, when reviewing the three Dutch periods, mainly regarded the role of the touch. In the Zaandam period, the brush describes the shape of things, as it were. There is a clear relation between the contours of the shape and the direction of the brush-strokes (figs. 60, 62). Sometimes vigorously, often in elongated touches, more or less delicately. What a difference from the Amsterdam paintings, where the strokes lead a life of their own, quite separate

52. Claude Monet, *The IJ, Amsterdam* (cat. no. 27).

from the shape. John House used the poetic image of butterflies fluttering through a garden, and that is often really what it looks like (figs. 58, 59, 61, 63).[40] Things are no longer 'described', but emerge from these patches. Right in the period in which these paintings were created, the group of artists to which Monet belonged were given the name of 'Impressionists', on account of his *Impression: soleil levant*. His touch is again more concrete in the paintings from the bulb-region (figs. 55-57). On these, the paint has often been deliberately applied so thickly that the light striking the 'walls' of the impasto is reflected, adding, as it were, a new source of light to the painting. The strokes of paint seem intertwined. This creates a remarkable web, which was further developed by Monet in his later years, e.g. in the famous series of grain stacks.

The colours also change. Precisely between the Zaandam period and the Amsterdam period, the colour black vanishes almost completely from Monet's palette.[41] It can still be found, whether blended or not, in the Zaandam paintings, especially in the landscapes with overcast skies (fig. 60). A lot of white was used for the light and intermediate hues, in that period (figs. 54, 62). Monet usually avoided painting dark shadows. He often had his back to the light, so that no visible shadows were cast by the elements of his motif. Thus, Monet profited from the discovery of the 'peinture claire'.[42] It had been discovered that light no longer had to exist by the grace of dark shadows, since the illusion of lightness could also be created by using light hues only and by the right arrangement of the colours. It has been shown, by the way, that the impressionists usu-

53. Claude Monet, *The Zuiddijk with the townhall and the Oostzijderkerk* (cat. no. 5).

54. Detail.

55. Claude Monet, *Bulb-fields and mills near Rijnsburg* (cat. no. 41).

56. Detail of cat. no. 41.

57. Detail of cat. no. 42.

ally exhibited their paintings against a dark background - as had been the tradition - thus creating a contrast between light and dark.[43] In those days, it was considered a dangerous adventure to enhance the power of colour, daring to confront contrasting colours. It was not a form of colouristic stylization, but it had to do with the growing awareness that tone and colour in the traditional art of painting had so much begun to obey laws of their own, that they only seemingly corresponded with reality. Anyone who dared admit that nature looked quite different from the paintings on his wall, almost felt a heretic.[44]

In 1887, Monet's friend and first biographer Théodore Duret described his vision (and probably Monet's as well) of the breakthrough of brighter colours as follows: 'We needed the arrival of Japanese albums in our midst before anyone dared to sit down on the bank of a river to juxtapose on a canvas a roof which was bright red, a white wall, a green poplar, a yellow road, and blue water. Before the example given by the Japanese this was impossible; the painter always lied. Nature with its bold colours blinded him; all one ever saw on a canvas were subdued colours drowning in a general half-tone.'[45] Reviewing Monet's Dutch oeuvre, this struggle for colour can clearly be felt. Sometimes it can be perceived how he went to extremes to render this colourful reality in all its garishness on his canvases (cat. nos. 7, 35).

Never satisfied

Eventually, Renoir was convinced that Monet had been right to persevere in plein-air painting; in a letter dated 1891, eight years after Renoir had given up painting outdoors consistently, he wrote: 'I have lost a lot of time by working within my four square meters of studio. I would have gained ten years by doing a little of what Monet has done.'[46] In spite of his statements on deceit when painting outdoors, Renoir had to agree that Monet was right. The unsuspecting observer of all these cheerful pictures is perhaps inclined to agree with Renoir and go on living with the image of the painter Monet, who, happily roaming the countryside, produced one

masterpiece after the other; two thousand times a truthful and colourful image of the world, 42 times of Zaandam, Amsterdam and the bulb-regions.[47] It sounds like a wonderful life, but the truth was different: looking back on his life, Monet said: 'Painting makes me suffer: all my old work with which I am not satisfied, and the impossibility of doing well every time. Yes, each time I begin a canvas, I hope to produce a masterpiece. I have every intention of it, and nothing comes out that way. Never to be satisfied – it is frightful.'[48] This discontent was, however, the driving power behind an enormous production of plein-air paintings, in an unrelenting effort to capture the fleeting reality. Although the Dutch paintings are only a small part of the oeuvre thus created, they cast an interesting light on Monet the painter, as well as on Dutch reality, a century ago.

* This article is based on research into thirteen Dutch paintings by Monet (cat. nos. 5, 9, 12, 16, 17, 18, 21, 25, 27, 28, 33, 41 en 42). I am very grateful to the owners and curators of these paintings for giving me the opportunity to study the works at length. It has been a privilege to discuss the results of my research with John House, of the Courtauld Institute of Art in London, and to verify them against the results of the comprehensive research which he has dedicated to Monet's working method for the past two decades. I am extremely grateful for having been allowed access to his book: *Claude Monet: Nature into Art*, New Haven & London 1986, which had not yet been published at the time. This enabled me to support my conclusions drawn from the examination of the paintings with numerous written sources and observations mentioned in his book. Since Monet's Dutch paintings have hardly come under review in his work, with this article I hope to provide a useful addition.

I owe a number of useful suggestions to a conversation with Anthea Callen, the author of: *Techniques of the Impressionists*, New Jersey 1982. I also thank the director of the Rijksmuseum Vincent van Gogh, Ronald de Leeuw, for giving me the opportunity to make the journeys required for my reseach. Finally, I thank my colleagues Karin van Nes and Vita Fontijn, and the trainees of the Central Research Laboratory for Objects of Arts and Science, Anneke Weersma, Maddie Baten, Evelyne Haarsma and Hélène Kat for their part in the research into the literature and the topographic research, and for their assistance with the editing and annotating of this article. The article was translated from the Dutch by Mandy Sikkens.

1. Ambroise Vollard, *La vie et l'oeuvre de Pierre Auguste Renoir*, Paris 1919, pp. 127-28; R. Régamey, 'La formation de Claude Monet', *Gazette des Beaux-Arts* 1927, pp. 65-84, p. 80 in particular.

2. Ambroise Vollard, *Paul Cézanne*, Paris 1915, p. 88.

3. Ludwig Richter, *Lebenserinnerungen eines deutschen Malers*, Leipzig 1947, pp. 186-87.

4. Renoir and Monet painted together several times; apart from studying together at the Academie Gleyre in 1862, they worked together in and around Fontainebleau in 1863; at Marlotte in 1865; at Paris (e.g. the Pont des Arts and the Champs-Elysées) in 1867; near Bougival, la Guinguette de la Grenouillère in 1869; at Argenteuil in 1872 and 1874; on the Rivièra in 1883. See François Daulte, *Auguste Renoir: Catalogue Raisonné*, Lausanne 1971, pp. 32, 35, 37, 49. For a comparison of the Grenouillère paintings by Monet and Renoir, see John House, *Claude Monet: Nature into Art*, New Haven & London 1986, pp. 52, 53.

5. Duc de Trévise, 'Le Pèlerinage de Giverny', *Revue de l'art* 1927, p. 122; see also: House, op. cit. (note 4), p. 135.

6. For sources regarding the history of plein-air painting, see House, op. cit. (note 4), pp. 135-47.

7. See House, op. cit. (note 4), p. 135.

8. See Appendix III, 5.

9. Verbal information from J.D. Bakker, Zaandam.

10. House, op. cit. (note 4), pp. 135-47.

11. The Zaandam paintings are about the same length (circa 73 cm) on the longer side. The lengths of the shorter sides vary between 34 to 54 cm. One of the Zaandam paintings (cat. no. 12) has been cut along the top edge, the paint of the sky continues on to the top edge of the canvas where it has been turned down, whereas the turned-down edges of the other paintings examined are only covered with a coat of primer. Monet's willingness to cut his canvases is shown in a diary note by René Gimpel, *Journal d'un Collectionneur*, Paris 1963, diary note on 28-11-1918.

12. Compare House, op. cit. (note 4), p. 155.

13. J. Rewald, 'Renoir and his Brother', *Gazette des Beaux-Arts* 27 (1945), p. 181.

14. In this connection, Renoir disparagingly told Ambroise Vollard about a painter who had rendered village scenes in which not a single person was to be seen. Renoir remarked on this, upon which the painter answered that no one had been walking in the streets while he was working there. See Vollard, op. cit. (note 2), p. 128.

15. Compare William C. Seitz, *Claude Monet*, New York 1960, fig. 10, 11, 15, 16, 21, 22, 40, 41, 42 and 43.

16. See House, op. cit. (note 4), pp. 15-33.

17. On Monet's choice of subjects when travelling, see House, op. cit. (note 4), pp. 23-24.

18. Appendix II, 3.

19. C. Pissarro, *Lettres à son fils Lucien*, ed. J. Rewald, Paris 1950, letter dated 3-2-1893.

20. According to M. Elder, *Chez Claude Monet à Giverny*, Paris 1924, Monet had bought his first Japanese prints as early as 1856; see also House, op. cit. (note 4), p. 47.

21. For Monet's use of studio-boats in Argenteuil, Vétheuil and Giverny, and the possible influence of Daubigny in this respect, see House, op. cit. (note 4), pp. 137-40.

22. Duc de Trévise, op. cit. (note 5), p. 126.

23. Upon counting the number of threads per centimetre, the canvases proved to have been painted on identical fabric.

24. G. de Maupassant, 'La vie d'un paysagiste', see House, op. cit. (note 4), p. 195.

25. Duc de Trévise, op. cit. (note 5), p. 126.

26. Paul Signac, *D'Eugène Delacroix au Neo-Impressionnisme*, Paris 1899, p. 54.

27. D. Hudson, *For Love of Painting: The life of Sir Gerald Kelly*, London 1975, p. 14; see also House, op. cit. (note 4), p. 144.

28. Appendix II, 4.

29. For a discussion of Monet's activities in the studio, see House, op. cit. (note 4), chapter 8.

30. Vollard, op. cit. (note 2), p. 128.

31. Daniel Wildenstein, *Claude Monet: Biographie et catalogue raisonné*, 4 volumes, Lausanne & Paris 1974-1985, vol. 2, letter no. 403.

32. Appendix II, 5.

33. Diary of the painter T. Robinson; Manuscript in the Boston Museum of Fine Arts, 23-5-1892.

34. Letter to Geffroy, dated 7-10-1890; Wildenstein, op. cit. (note 31), vol. 3, letter no. 1076; see also exhib. cat. *Monet: Painter of light*, Auckland (City Art Gallery) 1985, p. 23.

35. Manuscript at the Royal Library of Brussels, no. 15.552, published in part by M.P. Merrifield in: *Original Treatises on the Arts of Painting*, New York 1967 (reissue of edition printed in London 1849), pp. 766-840, pp. 824-25, in particular.

36. The various terms used in connection with the preliminary stages of French paintings in the nineteenth century are dealt with by A. Boime, *The Academy and French Painting in the Nineteenth Century*, New York 1971, pp. 79-89 in particular; House, op. cit. (note 4) deals with the terminology concerned, with particular emphasis on Monet on pp. 65-69 and 157-67.

37. On the various primers used by Monet, see House, op. cit. (note 4), pp. 63-65.

38. On Monet's painting technique, the following publications have been issued in the last few years: H. Adhémar, 'Modifications apportées par Monet à son Déjeuner sur l'herbe de 1865 à 1866', *Bulletin du laboratoire du Musée du Louvre* 1958, pp. 37-41; G. Sarraute, 'Contribution à l'étude du Dejeuner sur l'herbe de Monet', *Bulletin du laboratoire du Musée du Louvre* 1958, pp. 46-51; G. Bazin, 'Introduction à la technique des peintres impressionnistes', International Counsel of Museums 1969; M. Hours, 'Matière et manière impressionnistes', *Laboratoire de Recherche des Musées de France: Annales* 1974, pp. 5-34; S. Delbourgo et J.-P. Rioux, 'Contribution à l'étude de la matière picturale', *Laboratoire de Recherche des Musées de France: Annales* 1974, pp. 34-43; L. Faillant-Dumas, 'L'écriture picturale et la photographie', *Laboratoire de Recherche des Musées de France: Annales* 1974, pp. 43-64; B. Dunstan, *Painting methods of the impressionists*, New York 1976; E.H. Jones, *Monet unveiled: A new look at Boston's paintings*, Boston 1977, pp. 6-10; R. Herbert, 'Method and Meaning in Monet', *Art in America* 1979, pp. 90-108 (for a critical reaction to this article, see House, op. cit. (note 4), chap-

ter 5, note 30); M. Wilson, H. Wyld and A. Roy, 'Monet's Bathers at La Grenouillère', *National Gallery Technical Bulletin* 5 (1981); Anthea Callen, *Techniques of the impressionists*, New Jersey 1982.

39. J. Borely, 'Cézanne à Aix', in: *L'Art vivant*, July 1926.
40. House, op. cit. (note 4), p. 80.
41. Five more or less complete lists of the pigments or specifications of colours which Monet used on his palette, have been collected by House, op. cit. (note 4), p. 109. Monet told Gimpel, op. cit. (note 11), that he had already given up using black in his younger years; diary notes on 28-11-1918.
42. For an examination of the concept of 'peinture claire', see R. Shiff, *Cézanne and the end of Impressionism*, Chicago & London 1984, p. 199 etc.
43. House, op. cit. (note 4), p. 206.
44. See the contribution of Boudewijn Bakker, p. 28.
45. Théodore Duret, *Les peintres impressionnistes*, Paris 1878, pp. 65-68; see also House, op. cit. (note 4), p. 299.
46. Letter from Renoir to Durand-Ruel, dated 25-3-189 in: L. Venturi, *Les Archives de l'Impressionnisme*, Paris & New York 1939, vol. 1, p. 130.
47. Wildenstein has included 1963 paintings in his oeuvre-catalogue. We know, moreover, that Monet destroyed many paintings. In his younger years, by his own account, he slashed 200 paintings just before the arrival of the bailiff. See Gimpel, op. cit. (note 11), diary note on 28-10-1918. Durand-Ruel told Gimpel that Monet burned some London paintings from around 1900 and of his waterlily paintings. Diary note on 23-9-1927.
48. Gimpel, op. cit. (note 11), diary note on 28-11-1918.

58. Detail of cat. no. 27.

59. Detail of cat. no. 28.

60. Detail of cat. no. 18.

61. Detail of cat. no. 33.

62. Detail of cat. no. 9.

63. Detail of cat. no. 33.

'CLAUDE MONET'S DISCOVERY'. JAPANESE PRINTS GIVEN AWAY IN HOLLAND AS WRAPPING-PAPER?*

Joop M. Joosten

It is not out of place in this publication to devote some attention to the well-known tale of Monet's discovery of a pile of Japanese prints in a Zaandam grocery. I came across the story a number of years ago in the periodical *Op de Hoogte* 1912, where Tom Schilperoort alludes to it in connection with an exhibition of diverse Japanese art objects and curiosa in the Hilversum Public Library and Reading Room.[1] Schilperoort avails himself of the anecdote to make it clear that Japanese art was still awaiting discovery in the previous century, and to show how important this discovery was, when it came, for Europe: 'It was as if life thereby shed something of its complicated indirectness, becoming simpler, clearer, more intelligible and more beautiful'. Who would not become curious about those events in Zaandam which helped to give such a new turn to our lives?

The tale of Monet's find derives from Octave Mirbeau's *La 628-E8* of 1907, which consists of an assortment of reminiscences, fantasies and stories.[2] These are strung together as an account of a fictitious motoring trip through France, Belgium, Holland and Germany, the registration-number of the car in which the journey is made furnishing the title of the book. Octave Mirbeau (1848-1917), writer and art critic, is said to have known Monet as early as the mid-1880s. In 1886 they were in Noirmoutier together; after this Mirbeau wrote several times on Monet's work, which he greatly admired.

The story of the Japanese prints in Zaandam, which Mirbeau claims to have heard from the artist himself, comes up in an associative manner. Mirbeau is reminded of it when describing the little wooden bridges over the Dutch waterways, which evoke for him the image of Japanese prints (fig. 64). 'For the first time I became conscious of this oriental aspect, highly oriental, presented by most Dutch towns and villages, without its being precisely clear of what elements it is composed. They evoke at once the art of Japan and the primeval art of China, but also the art of the Indies and all the magic of continents bathed in water, and the Antilles, which Dutch ships have visited for hundreds of years, as if the seafarers had brought back from these lands beyond the far seas, together with the merchandise that made them wealthy, a moving reminder of how they looked.'[3] In such an Arabian Nights environment, and certainly in that of Zaandam, 'the most Japanese of all scenes in Holland', sooner or later a day was bound to come such as the 'enchanted day on which Claude Monet, having come to Holland, (...) found (...) the first Japanese print which he had ever set eyes upon.'[4]

This occurred after a visit to a grocer's, the artist suddenly noticing that the shopkeeper had wrapped up his purchases in Japanese prints. Amazed and elated at how beautiful they were, he rushed back in order to possess himself of the rest of the pile of 'wrapping-paper' lying on the counter. The shopkeeper turned out to be amenable to parting with his entire stock for nothing, seeing that the prints made poor wrapping-paper and besides, he discovered that he had some other, more suitable paper stored away. Mirbeau brings his story to a close with no mean claim: 'This was the beginning of a celebrated collection, but also (...) of such an evolution in French painting, at the close of the nineteenth century, that the anecdote, in addition to being colourful in its own right, retains genuine historical value. No-one wishing to

72

64. J. Barclay after Hildebrand, *View of Zaandam*. Zaandam, Municipal Archives.

make a serious study of this important artistic school, referred to as impressionism, can afford to ignore it.'[5]

When Mirbeau wrote his book he knew, of course, of Monet's interest in Japanese art of engraving. The mere fact that Monet had a large number of prints permanently hanging in the dining-room of his house at Giverny indicates that the painter made no secret of his taste. Mirbeau mentions one of the prints Monet acquired in Zaandam by name: *The Hinds* by Ogata Kō-rin, which is present in the artist's collection.[6]

But is it possible that this print, one of the oldest in his collection, could have been acquired by Monet in Holland as wrapping-paper? Does the story ring true? Whatever the answer may be to this question, Mirbeau's anecdote remains a striking illustration of the lack of interest on the part of the Dutch in Japanese art in general, and Japanese engravings in particular. This indifference would not be so remarkable in itself, were it not for the fact that – and I shall return to this later – there was an abundance of Japanese art and cultural artefacts in three public collections in Holland.

My proposition that Japanese art failed to interest the Dutch will meet with the immediate retort that Van Gogh's enthusiasm attests to the contrary. It is certainly true that in his letter of mid-January 1884 to his friend Furnée, Vincent mentions 'very beautiful things' which he had seen 'from China and Japan'. No sooner had he taken up residence in Antwerp, at the end of November 1885, than he pinned 'a group of little Japanese prints' to the wall of his new studio: 'small female figures in gardens or on the shore, horsemen, flowers, gnarled thorn branches'. Moreover, in the letter in which he mentions them to Theo he quotes, approvingly, 'one of De Goncourt's sayings': 'japonaiserie for ever'.[7] But rather than undermining the proposition, I would suggest that this evidence actually corroborates it. For this is the first time that a Dutch artist expressed himself so directly and so positively on the subject of Japanese prints, a good fourteen years after Monet's 'enchanted day'.

A few words are in order at this point concerning the situation in France. A number of different dates are given for the discovery there of the Japanese art of engraving, all being in the region of 1860. The etcher Felix Braquemond, the poet Charles Baudelaire and the writers Jules and Edmond de Goncourt are variously mentioned as the discoverers. In 1868, the critic Zacharie Astruc was able to grace his article 'Le

Japon chez nous' in the French periodical *l'Etendard* with eighteen names of prominent French devotees of Japanese art. It should be noted that this was more than seventeen years before Van Gogh's allusion to his 'group of little Japanese prints'. The last name on the list is that of Monet, with the epithet 'a faithful emulator of Hokusai'.[8] So in contrast to what Mirbeau tells us, it is an established fact that Monet knew of a special Japanese art of print making long before coming to Holland.

Japanese cultural artefacts in Holland

The crucial role played by the Republic of the United Provinces (and after the Napoleonic period, The Netherlands) in the relationship between Japan and Europe has often been noted. For two hundred years the artificial peninsula of Deshima joined by a bridge to the Nagasaki coast, was practically the only gate through which goods from Japan passed to be shipped to Europe, and through which the Dutch representatives, as the sole Europeans there, came into direct contact with the Japanese world. Our interest here is less in these goods than in the personal property and mementos the Dutch brought back from this strange, distant land. For such personal belongings were more truly Japanese than the official merchandise, which was essentially European with Japanese covers: i.e. *Japonaiserie* along the same lines as the chinoiserie of the eighteenth century. Given the severe, monopolistic restrictions on exporting from Japan, these authentic Japanese articles must have been very few in number.

The last-mentioned state of affairs was changed somewhat by the return of Isaac Titsingh (1740-1812), who was chief of the trading-post on Deshima from 1778 to 1784. He is assumed to have been the first man to bring back a large collection of Japanese objects, when he returned from Deshima in 1809, one which must have been built up with care. However, few people knew about it. It was not publicized until 1893 when Titsingh's heir, J.D.C. Titsingh, sold it by auction in order to make room for his expanding collection of modern

65. W. Hekking Jr., *Main group of the section: Japanese religion*. From: *Nederlandsch Magazijn* 1863.

art. The auction catalogue lists ceramics, netsukes, bronzes, lacquer-ware, kakemonos, prints and books totalling 622 lots.[9] A second, similar collection, of items accumulated by Hendrik Doeff, who led the post on Deshima from 1804 to 1817, was lost by shipwreck on the way to Holland.[10]

J. Cock Blomhoff (1779-1853), Doeff's successor as chief of the Deshima post from 1816 to 1823, was more fortunate. Not only did his collection arrive intact, but it was bought by the State in 1826 and assigned to the Mauritshuis in The Hague, finally coming to rest in the Cabinet of Rarities, which had been housed in the ground floor rooms of the museum since 1821. There it was joined, in 1831, by J.G.F. van Overmeer Fischer's collection. Fischer (1800-1848) had been the warehouseman on Deshima from 1825-1829.[11]

In order to gain an impression of the exhibits we must resort to documentary sources. Something in the nature of a description of the Cabinet's contents may be found in

Van der Aa's Geographical dictionary of 1843: 'in five connecting rooms, an unimaginable wealth of diverse objects of all manner of kinds, and which may be regarded as the most important of contributions to (our knowledge of) sacred and civil ceremonies, the customs, traditions, means of livelihood and mode of recreation of people dwelling overseas, and more in particular of the Chinese and Japanese. Thus the first two rooms contain the objects from China, the third those from Japan, the fourth has items from every continent, whilst the fifth is reserved for the consignment of Dutch rarities and artistic objects.'[12]

The exhibits are listed after the manner of a catalogue in an undated guide by the curator of the time, A.A. van de Kasteele.[13] However, it is striking that neither Van der Aa nor Van de Kasteele speaks of the paintings and prints belonging to the two collections. Were they not displayed? Or did both men consider them to be negligible?

But however remarkable the Cabinet, and however many precious and rare objects it may have housed, the curator of the Leyden Museum van Oudheden wrote in an essay of 1860 that it did not constitute 'even a remotely complete survey of that which we require, in order to build up an accurate and vivid picture of the customs, conventions and traditions, the level of civilisation and scientific development pertaining to the inhabitants.' The items exhibited were 'more suited to the satisfaction of idle curiosity and casual enjoyment than that of the thirst for sound knowledge and thorough instruction.'[14]

The Cabinet remained in the Mauritshuis until 1875. Then it was moved to the premises of 15 Lange Vijverberg, where the collection may have been seen by Van Gogh. In 1883 the Cabinet was closed, the ethnographic section being transferred to Leyden where it was assigned to the National Ethnographic Museum.

The National Von Siebold Japanese Museum in Leyden

Whereas the collections of Cock Blomhoff and Overmeer Fischer doubtless came about by the haphazard acquisition of Japanese curiosa, after 1823 collecting became a somewhat more academic and professional matter, with the arrival of the physician Dr. Ph. F. von Siebold (1796-1866) on Deshima. Von Siebold apparently took it upon himself to make his collection as complete as possible. Henceforth, not only would the interested man in the street in Holland be enabled to gain a good impression of the lives and way of thinking of the Japanese people, but the scholar, too, would have a sound apparatus at his disposal for the development of a science of ethnography, and finally the government would have access to a panoply of suggestions from the most reliable of sources, for ways in which trade could be broadened. On his return to Holland in 1830 Von Siebold immediately set about converting his house at the top of the Rapenburg in Leyden into a Japanese museum. He was soon also endeavouring to persuade the State to buy his collection, so that he would be able to finance his continuing research. In 1836 this plan succeeded, and the National Von Siebold Japanese Museum had become a reality.[15]

However, the collection was not destined to enjoy a peaceful existence. A mere two years later, Von Siebold let the ground floor of his house to a students' club, with all the attendant inconvenience and loss of space for the exhibition. In 1847 he was even obliged to sell his house, and the collection was moved to far more cramped quarters in Paardensteeg, now called Prinsessekade, where it remained until 1859. This accommodation must have left a great deal to be desired. The situation had become insupportable by the time Von Siebold left Leyden in 1859, the curator of the Museum van Oudheden, C. Leemans being designated to replace him. Leemans tackled the problem vigorously, and within a year the collection was re-housed in a new building in Breestraat with better facilities.

In these new premises the collection was arranged in the way Von Siebold had devised. Once again we are without illustrations and must be content with written records. We have Leemans' report mentioned earlier, written in May 1860 after the opening of the collection.

66. August Allebé, *Japanese dummies,* 1881. Amsterdam, Municipal Museum. Allebé's comment: 'I used some Japanese dummies when I decided to try a Japanese theme, but of course nothing came of it. These two can be mounted with the smaller one filling te blank space, the blue less harsh than it is here would be best, I think.'

After publication in the *Nederlandsche Staats-Courant* this article reappeared in *De Tijdstroom*, a monthly magazine, which later issued it as a visitor's guide. It enables us to acquire a reasonable picture of what was shown in this new museum.[16]

According to Leemans, Von Siebold had divided the collection into four major sections: 1. 'scientific objects, manuscripts, books, drawings, prints, coins and some few antiquities'; 2. 'products of the country, of the industry of the inhabitants, arts and crafts'; 3. 'models of buildings, ships, implements, tools and household articles, in some cases these implements and tools themselves'; 4. objects etc. 'from re-gions under tribute to Japan or annexed to that country, as well as those of other peoples and lands', together constituting a section 'devoted to comparative Ethnography.'[17]

There were many separate drawings on display. These were distributed over all the exhibition rooms, along the walls or freely hanging from the ceiling. The subjects were arranged to correspond with the surrounding exhibits. Thus the following could be seen: 'pictures of *sacred subjects,* of gods, priests, monks, temples, chapels, ceremonies and festivals; of *customs and traditions,* customs, trades, agriculture, fishing and hunting, ground plans of gardens and villas, crafts, handiwork and implements, weapons and ships. *Landscapes,* land and sea views. (...) Drawings constituting *proof of artistic excellence produced by living artists* in Japan in 1823-1830, including a collection of drawings by the most celebrated masters in Yedo and sketches made by the so-called *lightning artists.* Drawings made *on festive occasions* and at *traditional ceremonies* of an historical or religous nature, portraits, landscapes, animal- and flower-pieces as well as mixed forms; drawings which were hung *as gifts in the Shinto temples,* and drawings on *church banners, draught screens, fans* etc. (...) The value of this collection, unique in its kind, is increased by virtue of its proceeding not only from the nature of the objects displayed but also from the largely superb workmanship, on account of which the drawings may also be regarded as proof of artistic excellence. A great number of these, which

distinguish themselves also in this latter respect, drawn on silk by the hand of masters of wide renown, are even purchased in Japan with gold. The views of Yedo by the court painter Hoksaï and those of the famous Mount Fujiyama by Tekkaï of Ohosaka deserve especial mention; whilst a series of drawings from nature of crabs and insects by the artist Tetsan, also executed on silk, are among the finest that Japan has produced'.[18]

Again, there is no mention in this list of the substantial collection of prints and illustrated books owned by the museum. There may be a passing allusion to it under the heading 'products of arts and crafts' where we find the words: 'paper and objects made from paper, books, wood-cuts, bookbinding, a great variety of samples of paper of all kinds and patterns.'[19]

In the very same year the museum was further endowed with the eighteen six-part screens presented to King William III by the then Shogun of Japan. Before these screens were turned over to the museum they were displayed to an admiring general public in the Leyden municipal concert-hall during the month of April 1860.

The National Von Siebold Japanese Museum was evidently situated in Breestraat until 1883. In 1864, however, the name was changed to the National Ethnographic Museum. In the reorganisations of 1883 the Chinese and Japanese collections of both Leyden and The Hague were brought together in the house at 67 Rapenburg.

The Museum of Japanese Rarities in Amsterdam

Far-reaching political and social developments and upheavals in Japan followed in the wake of the naval actions under the American Commodore M.C. Perry in 1853/1854. Japan was forced to open its borders to the outside world, and this naturally had repercussions on the relationship between Japan and Holland. Although the Dutch government was anxious to maintain Holland's privileged trading position in Japan there was no choice but to relinquish

67. George Hendrik Breitner, *Girl in white kimono*. Enschedé, Rijksmuseum Twenthe.

the initiative, making it the prerogative of private enterprise. The trading-rights, from 1858 onwards, were exercised by the Dutch Trading Company, settled in Amsterdam. In order to be able to adapt to the new situation and to gain the confidence of the Japanese, the Company's directors asked Von Siebold to investigate the situation in Japan and to introduce them at the court of the Shogun. One of the results of Von Siebold's second journey was another Japanese collection in the same vein as the first. A year after his return in 1862, it was displayed as the 'Japanese Exhibition' in the rooms of the Amsterdam Society for National Industry which had invited Von Siebold to show his collection there (fig. 65). The latter had the opportunity 'to present to the mercantile public and those practising the arts and sciences in the capital city of Holland, the proof of the results of my scholarly researches in general and more specifically those into arts, crafts and products suitable for exportation, for their inspection and appraisal, and above all, as a means of encouragement to the Dutch trade which has been established in that land for centuries. To the extent that the 'Japanese exhibition' is favourably characterised by objects of exceeding rarity and of great importance for science and for the arts and crafts, this has been made possible by the invitation of the *Taikun* for me to visit his capital city, Yedo, and by my relations with dignitaries, with scholars and artists – my friends.'[20]

This time, Von Siebold's attempts to interest the State in purchasing the collection failed.[21] Although the annual reports of the Royal Amsterdam Zoological Society, Natura Artis Magistra, which had founded an ethnographical museum in the zoological gardens two years earlier, indicate that the Society seriously considered buying the collection, the negotiations bore no fruit.'[22] At this, Von Siebold had it transported to Germany, where its destination proved to be the Museum für Völkerkunde in Munich.

In spite of this, the Society Artis Natura Magistra was able to acquire such a large number of 'rarities related to the customs and traditions of the Japanese people', during the

following decade, that this collection had an entire room to itself in 1876. In terms of content this Museum of Japanese Rarities' did not differ from the Cabinet in the Hague and the Leyden museum.[23] In 1921 it was transferred, together with the rest of the Society's ethnographical museum, to the Associated Colonial Institute, which placed the collections in the Colonial Museum, opened in 1923, the present Tropenmuseum.

The interest shown by the Dutch art world

It is clear that in 1871, when Monet came to Holland, Japan was quite conspicuously present here. Without too much difficulty it was possible, in this country, to become reasonably conversant with Japanese art and culture. Firstly there were the above-mentioned public collections of Japanese objects, and secondly, those interested could avail themselves of various publications issued by regular travellers to and from Deshima, which had appeared at constant intervals on the Dutch market since the 1820s.

It is not until reading of the inordinate difficulty with which French enthusiasts procured information on Japanese art that we become aware of how extremely favourable the Dutch situation was in the 1860s and 1870s. And yet who was there in the art world to sit up and take notice (fig. 66)? Until now, I have been able to trace only one representative, and this is someone whose interest was aroused not in Holland but in France. It is the painter David Adolph Constant Artz, of whom P.A. Haaxman Jr. wrote in the *Elsevier's Geïllustreerd Maandschrift* of 1898: 'During Artz's stay in Paris, Japanese art reigned surpreme. The passion for things Japanese permeated the entire art world, expressing itself not only in the collection of trinkets and in the interior decoration of people's homes with Japanese furniture, but also in the subjects chosen by artists. In this period Artz painted several genre pieces *à la Japonaise,* i.e. Parisian figures in Japanese surroundings with beautifully-coloured materials and draperies.'[24] In the auction catalogue of Artz's estate, which was exhibited and sold by auction in 1891, in the hall of the Pulchri Studio society of artists in The Hague, lot 144 is described as 'eight Japanese prints' and lot 155 'Two small Japanese illustrated books' which he had apparently purchased during his stay in Paris.[25] Just how unorthodox Artz's taste was, is evident from the fact that his friends Jacob and Matthijs Maris, who were also living in Paris at the time, were not the least bit charmed by Japanese art, though Artz will certainly have directed their attention to its excellence.

Without exaggerating, Carel Vosmaer could begin his review of Louis Gonse's *l'Art Japonais* of 1883 in the following way: 'In England, Germany and France, there has long been recognition for Chinese and especially for Japanese art as *art*, and for some years they have also been included as such in museums of art. In our country there is still too great a tendency to classify the Chinese and Japanese objects, as has been the practice since the seventeenth century, as 'curiosities'; the fact that they have been the object of thorough study on the part of some individuals, as a source of knowledge and illumination for ethnography, was already a great step forwards. However, with few exceptions the vast majority regard the products of the Far East as oddities, and anyone seriously affirming the great significance of Chinese and especially Japanese art, is still deprecatingly referred to as a 'queer Chinaman.''[26]

He was not to know that the tide was turning among the younger generation of artists. This changing taste would not manifest itself until the latter half of the 1880s, and then as part of a more general inclination for matters oriental (fig. 67). Specific appreciation for the Japanese art of printmaking was not widespread until about 1890, the impulse coming from France rather than Holland.

'Claude Monet's Discovery'

Was Monet aware, we may wonder, of the presence of all these Japanese cultural artefacts in Holland? Any Frenchman with greater than superficial interest would have known of the age-old close relationship between Holland and Japan. Furthermore, such a person would have been able to find references, in studies of any depth, to treatises published by Thunberg, Titsingh and Von Siebold, which were also accessible to a French readership.

'The main works are said to be in The Hague' notes Astruc in his article on Japanese art in *l'Etendart* of 1867.[27] 'Said' by whom? At least three French 'japonistes' are known to have visited the Leyden museum. On 14 September 1861 the De Goncourt brothers noted in their diary that they had visited the National Japanese Museum in Leyden: 'At the Siebold Museum, rough sketches in ink by Japanese artists, which have the picturesque spirit and dashes of a Fragonard bistre.' Although they had visited the Mauritshuis the day before, there was no diary entry concerning the Cabinet of Rarities.[28]

There is, in fact, an amusing little story proving how well-informed they were as to Japanese objects in Holland. The painter Philippe Zilcken from The Hague thought he might be able to provide Edmond with an illuminating piece of information in reaction to the latter's article on Japanese art in the *Figaro*. He must have been startled, to say the least, at receiving the following reply from De Goncourt:

March 27th, '81
Monsieur. Thank you for the kind sentiments that prompted you to write to me, but please understand that this opinion was not advanced lightly. I have been studying Japan for thirty years, I have seen the Museum in the Hague, and aside from the lacquer-ware, the kakemonos and such kakemonos as we do not have in Europe, and lastly the porcelain referred to as old Japan, all the other items seem to me to be imitations of Chinese art, whilst Japanese art, nature seen through Japanese eyes, does not begin until O-Kou-sai. Thus the statue which is indisputably the finest possessed by M. Chernuschi is from the time of Louis XVI, or possibly the Directory, the bronzes similar to the wax of To-oun and Sei-Muo are by bronze artists who have only been dead for forty of fifty years, etc. etc., but one

ought to read the pages I have devoted to justifying this view, which will be contested because it reverses received opinion but which I believe to be true as a general thesis, very true.
Assuring you of my most considered attention, I remain, respectfully yours.

Edmond de Goncourt.[29]

When Zilcken visited Paris, not long after this, there was another surprise in store for him. At Desoye's, the leading art dealer in Japanese objects in the Rue de Rivoli, he was not only given the address of De Goncourt, whom Mme Desoye described as having the same taste as Zilcken, but also the information that she had sold him 'many things that she had brought back with her after a long stay in Japan, *where she had also met Von Siebold.*'[30]

In addition to the De Goncourt brothers, Louis Gonse also paid a visit to the Leyden collection. In his *l'Art Japonais* of 1883 he writes: 'The library at Leyden today houses the finest and most precious collection of illustrated Japanese books in the world.' And in the reprint of 1886: 'The Ethnographic Museum in Leyden houses a collection of seven or eight hundred Kakemonos brought back by Siebold, some of which are of the most outstanding quality.'[31]

It remains very much an open question, going by these few observations, whether Monet had any idea of the cultural artefacts to be seen in Holland. Without dismissing Mirbeau's story – to come back to it at this point – as belonging to the realm of literary fables, I do find it highly questionable. The harder one tries to imagine the way in which those prints ended up on the counter in Zaandam, the more improbable the story becomes. How large was the pile? Were there ten, twenty, fifty, a hundred prints? How could anyone have acquired such a pile of prints at the time? Can it be a coincidence that there is also a traditional story about the very first Japanese prints and illustrated books in France being used as wrapping-paper? Is it not possible that Monet bought a few prints at a bookseller's or a print-shop, prints which had been sold by someone returning from De-

shima?[32] Considering how little interest there was in Holland, they certainly would not have cost much. The price may have been so low that in Paris it would have only bought you, in a manner of speaking, the paper itself. And who would not feel, with such a windfall, that it was an 'enchanted day'?

* The article was translated from the Dutch by Bev Jackson.
1. Tom Schilperoort, 'Over den invloed der Japansche kunst en haar nut', *Op de Hoogte* 9 (1912), pp. 461-65.
2. Octave Mirbeau, *La 628-E8*, Paris 1907, pp. 206-10. The 1977 re-issue is reviewed by Rudy Kousbroek in the Cultural Supplement of the *NRC/Handelsblad* of 2 October 1981: 'Xerox-E: de Japanse prenten van Claude Monet.'
3. Ibid., p. 207.
4. Ibid., p. 207.
5. Ibid., p. 209.
6. Geneviève Aitken and Marianne Delafond, *La Collection d'estampes japonaises de Claude Monet à Giverny*, Giverny 1983, cat no. 196.
7. *The complete letters of Vincent van Gogh*, 2 vols., London, 1958, vol. 2, letter 351a, p. 255; vol. 2, letter 437, p. 431. The present translation is a revised one.
8. Zacharie Astruc, 'Le Japon chez nous', *l'Etendard* 26 May 1868; quoted by Sharon Fletcher in: *Zacharie Astruc: Critic, Artist and Japoniste*, New York & London 1978, p. 360.
9. Cat. *l'Art japonais, La collection du Dr. J. Titsingh à la Haye*, Amsterdam (Frederik Muller) 12 April 1893 (Frits Lugt, *Repertoire des catalogues de ventes publiques intéressant l'art et la curiosité*, 3 vols., The Hague 1938-64, vol. 3, no. 51598).
10. Hendrik Doeff, *Herinneringen uit Japan*, Haarlem 1833.
11. Th. H. Lunsingh Scheurleer, 'Het Koninklijk Kabinet van Zeldzaamheden en zijn betekenis voor het Rijksmuseum', *Bulletin Koninklijke Nederlandse Oudheidkundige Bond* 9 (1956), pp. 270-308; F.J. Duparc, *Een eeuw strijd voor Nederlands cultureel erfgoed*, The Hague 1975, pp. 57, 123-25. See also P.H. Pott, *Naar wijder horizon*, The Hague n.d.
12. A.J. van der Aa, *Aardrijkskundig Woordenboek der Nederlanden*, vol. 4, Gorinchem 1843, pp. 790-91.
13. A.A. van de Kasteele, *Korte Handleiding ter bezichtiging der verzameling van zeldzaamheden in het Koninklijk Kabinet op het Mauritshuis in 's-Gravenhage*, The Hague n.d..
14. C. Leemans, 'Rijks Japansch Museum Von Siebold', *Nederlandsche Staats-Courant*, 9 May 1860; reprinted in *De Tijdstroom* 3 (1860), vol. 2, pp. 204-19 (p. 204 quotation), and as a brochure entitled *Korte Handleiding bij het bezigtigen van het Rijksmuseum Von Siebold*, The Hague 1860.
15. Leemans, op. cit. (note 14). See also C.C.F.M. le Roux, *Overzicht van de geschiedenis van het Rijksmuseum voor Volkenkunde 1837-1937. Gedenkschrift uitgege-*

ven bij de heropening van het museum op den 30sten November 1937, Leiden n.d.; and Duparc, op. cit. (note 11), pp. 63 and 134-39. On Von Siebold, see Bijleveld, 'Verloren glorie. Jhr. Dr. F. von Siebold en zijn buitenplaats Nippon', *Leids Jaarboekje* 17 (1920), pp. 102-29; the Siebold issue of *Nieuws uit Japan*, Spring 1977, with articles by various authors; Yu-Ying Brown, 'The Von Siebold collection from Tokugawa Japan', *The British Library Journal* 1 (1975), pp. 163-70 and ibid., 2 (1976), pp. 38- 55.

16. See note 14.
17. Ibid., p. 209 (brochure p. 16).
18. Ibid., p. 212 (brochure p. 19).
19. Ibid., p. 214 (brochure p. 21).
20. *Handleiding bij het bezichtigen der verzameling voorwerpen (...) bijeengebracht door Jhr. Ph. F. von Siebold in 1859-1862*, Amsterdam 1863. See also P.H. Witkamp, 'De tentoonstelling van Japansche voorwerpen te Amsterdam', *Nederlandsch Magazijn* 1863, pp. 377-79.
21. Lunsingh Scheurleer, op. cit. (note 11), p. 295.
22. See also P.H. Witkamp, *Natura Artis Magistra*, no place of publication given 1864, p. 48 note 1.
23. R.T. Mailand, 'Ontstaan, ontwikkeling en bloei van het Koninklijk Zoölogisch Genootschap Natura Artis Magistra te Amsterdam', *Bijdrage tot de Dierkunde* 1888, anniversary edition, p. 21. See also J.E. Rombouts, *Artis: Kijkjes in de dierentuin*, Amsterdam n.d., pp. 403-4.
24. P.H. Haaxman Jr., 'David Adolphe Constant Artz', *Elsevier's Geïllustreerd Maandschrift* 8 (1898), vol. 15, pp. 304-5.
25. Cat. *Atelier Adolphe Artz*, The Hague (Boussod, Valadon & Cie) 27-28 January 1891 (Lugt, op. cit. (note 9), vol. 3, no. 495993). No. 219 gives the description of a 'double Japanese screen' and no. 221 has a 'Japanese dress, light green, embroidered with flowers'.
26. *De Nederlandsche Spectator* 1883, pp. 379-80; 'queer chinaman' ('een rare chinees') is a common Dutch expression meaning, approximately, ' queer customer'.
27. Quoted by Fletscher, op. cit. (note 8), p. 349, note 33.
28. *Edmond et Jules de Goncourt: Journal,* vol. 4, Paris 1956, pp. 239-40.
29. Ph. Zilcken, 'Quelques souvenirs sur Edmond de Goncourt', *La Revue de Hollande* 1 (1915), vol. 2, pp. 61-66. See also Ph.Z. Zilcken, 'Edmond de Goncourt', *Elsevier's Geïllustreerd Maandschrift* 6 (1896), vol. 12, pp. 222-33.
30. Unpublished autobiography of Philippe Zilcken in the *Rijksbureau voor Kunsthistorische Documentatie* in The Hague, p. 22.
31. Louis Gonse, *l'Art japonais*, Paris 1883, vol. 2, p. 339; idem, *l'Art japonais*, Paris 1886.
32. As I was finishing this article, the following interesting piece of information came my way. In her essay 'Documentary Evidence for the Availability of Japanese Imagery in Europe in Nineteenth-Century Public Collections', *Art Bulletin* 86 (1986), pp. 110-11, Phyllis Floyd notes that the Bibliothèque Nationale in Paris owns a number of Japanese illustrated books and prints which were acquired in 1855, from the Dutch historian and man of letters U.G. Lauts (1787-1865).

MONET AND THEO VAN GOGH*

Ronald Pickvance

That Theo van Gogh played an important role as *engagé* dealer, enthusiastic supporter and loyal friend of many of the major Impressionist and Post-Impressionist painters has long been recognized (fig. 68). Warm tributes were paid to his advocacy of their work by both Gauguin and Pissarro. Fortunately, the Paris stock books of Boussod, Valadon et Cie, successors of Goupil, have survived, enabling the historian to follow the pattern of Theo's purchases from 1884 to October 1890. John Rewald's invaluable study, *'Theo van Gogh, Goupil and the Impressionists'*, published in 1973, has made such an assessment possible.[1]

During the later half of the 1880s, Theo handled work of Degas, Guillaumin, Monet, Pissarro, Renoir and Sisley among the Impressionists; and of Cézanne, Gauguin, Redon and Toulouse-Lautrec among the Post-Impressionists. Of these ten artists, Monet's paintings far outnumbered the rest. The Boussod Valadon stock books reveal that Theo purchased 3 Renoirs, none of them bought from the artist; 3 Guillaumins, all from the artist; 9 Sisleys, 5 from the artist; 20 Degas, 14 from the artist; 20 Pissarros, 18 from the artist: a total of 55 Impressionist works. Theo also bought 1 Cézanne (not from the artist), 1 Redon, 1 Toulouse-Lautrec and 11 Gauguins: that is 14 Post-Impressionist works. In all, 69 works from nine artists. By an extraordinary coincidence, Theo had through his hands at least 69 paintings by Monet, of which 42 came directly from the painters's studio.[2]

Proportionately, Theo worked as unremittingly for Monet as for the rest of the artists, organizing sales to collectors and exhibitions of his work that resulted in significant critical write-ups. He sold the vast majority of the paintings that he purchased. He arranged two important exhibitions in his small gallery on the Boulevard Montmartre, the first in June 1888, the second in February-March 1889. And it was Theo's enterprise and initiative that led to an exhibition of twenty works by Monet at the London branch of Boussod and Valadon (where it was still known as Goupil) in April-May 1889. Theo's Paris exhibitions provoked some of the most timely and perceptive criticism from two of Monet's most zealous advocates, Gustave Geffroy and Octave Mirbeau.

The artist-art dealer relationship, coldly documented in the firm's ledgers, can now be seen in a warmer light with the publication here of eight surviving letters from Monet to Theo van Gogh belonging to the Vincent van Gogh Foundation. Between April 1887 and October 1890, Monet probably wrote some twenty letters to Theo. Perhaps the missing ones were absorbed into the Boussod Valadon files, and are now lost. Not one of Theo's replies has been preserved.

The two men probably met in April 1887, almost a year after Monet's last visit to Holland to paint the bulb fields. Monet had recently quarrelled with Durand-Ruel, his major dealer since 1872. He strongly disagreed with Durand-Ruel's attempts to enter the American market. Monet no longer exhibited with the Impressionists, particularly at their eighth and final group show of 1886. Instead, he had chosen, since 1885, to show in the more fashionable and stylistically eclectic summer exhibition organized by Georges Petit. Theo's arrival on the scene meant that Monet now had a new dealer to play off against Petit and Durand-Ruel.

68. *Theo van Gogh*, c. 1889. Photo: Rijksmuseum Vincent van Gogh (Vincent van Gogh Foundation).

As a result of their first meeting, Theo bought two Belle-Ile paintings of 1886. They were entered in the stockbook on 7 April 1887. By 20 April Theo had sold both.[3] He wrote to Monet that day, telling him so. One of these was sold in part-exchange for a Degas, which Monet clearly coveted. This was almost certainly *La Femme à la Toilette,* a pastel over monotype, and the only Degas Monet owned.[4] Replying to Theo on 21 April, Monet referred to the sale of the Belle-Ile paintings, to the despatch of the Degas pastel to Giverny, and to his sending back to Paris another painting of Belle-Ile that Theo had indicated he wished to buy.

Giverny par Vernon eure

Cher Monsieur,
Je m'empresse de vous répondre que le tableau que vous me demandez est à vous.
Si le cadre du Degas est prêt, voulez-vous être assez aimable de me l'expédier en gare de Vernon au tard parce qu'il me tarde d'un jour, et puis vous pourrez faire faire l'emballage juste assez grand pour

que je puisse vous retourner dans la même caisse le tableau de Belle ile. Et je pense pas pouvoir venir à Paris avant le 4 ou 5 mai, ce qui m'empêchera à mon grand regret de pouvoir vous montrer ce que je compte exposer.
J'ai beaucoup à travailler et si je puis terminer quelque nouvelle chose, ce ne sera qu'en travaillant jusqu'au dernier moment.
Ainsi pourriez-vous disposer d'un instant et venir jusqu'à Giverny. Enfin écrivez-moi au sujet du Degas et ce que je dois faire pour votre tableau.
Je suis enchanté que vous avez si rapidement vendu un de mes tableaux et j'espère que cela va marcher de mieux en mieux.
Recevez mes compliments distingués
Claude Monet
21 avril 87

Theo responded immediately by paying his first *documented* visit to Giverny on 22 April. We learn of this in Monet's letter to Georges Petit of 23 April: 'You know it's going very well with the firm of Boussod (...) Mr. van Gogh came here yesterday to tell me that he had already sold one *Mer de Belle Ile*, and to ask me again for others, so he has six of them, four of which he intends to exhibit.'[5] Theo presumably took with him the Degas pastel, and brought back the Belle-Ile picture, which was entered into to the stockbook the following day.

The business relationship was set in motion. By the end of 1887, he had bought thirteen more canvases from Monet, eight of them of Belle-Ile.[6] (For Theo, 1887 was essentially the year of the Belle-Ile paintings; in all, he purchased eleven). This remarkable development cannot be followed in any detail: regrettably, Monet's letters to Theo are lost. But it was largely thanks to Theo that Monet was able to write to Théodore Duret on 7 November 1887: 'In Paris, things couldn't be going better for me, even beyond my expectations, and I should be extremely pleased if I could be as satisfied with my paintings.'[7]

Even more regrettable is the loss of all the letters Monet wrote Theo from Antibes in 1888,

69. Claude Monet, *A bend in the river Epte at Giverny*, 1888. Philadelphia, Philadelphia Museum of Art, William L. Elkins Collection.

where he painted from late January to the end of April. Monet's letters to Alice Hoschedé allow some glimpses: how Theo's purchase of a painting of Bennecourt eased their financial situation; and how Theo asked for first refusal on the Antibes paintings.[8] Once back in Giverny in early May, Monet was visited by Theo. 'You will see some lovely things at Claude Monet's', Vincent van Gogh wrote to his brother on about 7 May.[9] By 4 June, ten Antibes landscapes were bought by Theo. John Rewald has observed: 'Monet received between 1.000 and 1.300 frs for each canvas, according to size (the total amounted to 11.900 frs), but in addition was promised a 50-50 division of the profits. Thus, the artist did not give anything on con-

signment yet did not request an unreasonable outlay of cash either. When seven of the ten paintings were sold that very year and the other three during the following one, the benefits to be shared reached 27.720 frs – probably minus some expenses – of which the painter's portion must have been about 13.000 frs, on an average of 2.500 per picture.'[10]

This arrangement, by which Monet shared half of the profits, must have formed part of an agreement drawn up between the artist and Boussod and Valadon that also gave the dealers first refusal on all his paintings. Monet refers to this agreement in a letter to Durand-Ruel of 24 September.[11]

Perhaps, above all, the loss of Monet's let-

70. Claude Monet, *Landscape with figures, Giverny*, 1888.
Whereabouts unknown.

ters to Theo deprives us of his reactions to the
exhibition of the ten Antibes canvases. Theo arranged this in his small Boulevard Montmartre
gallery in June 1888. And in that month alone,
five of the paintings were sold. The exhibition
brought an ecstatic review from Gustave Geffroy in *La Justice* of 17 June.[12] Theo sent a copy
of this review to his brother in Arles, who responded immediately: 'I have just read Geffroy's article on Claude Monet. What he says is
really very good. I should so like to see that
exhibition.'[13] On about 17 June, Theo also
wrote to Monet about the Geffroy review,
which then prompted the artist to write to the
critic: 'I have just received a note from van
Gogh who tells me about the article you have
written concerning his exhibition; apparently it
is very good and I should quite like to read it.
(Please be kind enough to send it to me.) (...)
Van Gogh seems triumphant to me.'[14]

Theo again visited Giverny in late September, apparently without buying any paintings. But his enormous success with the Antibes
landscapes clearly enabled Monet to affirm on 1
October that 'my position and affairs are most
satisfactory.'[15] However, it was Valadon alone
who next visited Giverny in December. But it

was to Theo, not Valadon, that Monet wrote on
29 December. Theo had just returned to Paris
after visiting Vincent in Arles following his
breakdown.

Giverny par Vernon eure

Cher Monsieur Van gogh
Je suis en train de terminer les deux ta-
bleaux choisis par Mr Valadon. Je vous les
apporterai lundi matin. Serai chez vous
vers 10 hrs. faites votre possible pour vous
y trouver.
Compliments
Claude Monet
29 Déc 88

In fact, not just two, but seven paintings were
bought and entered in the stockbook on Monday 31 December 1888, immediately after
Monet's visit to Theo.[16] These pictures were acquired on the same terms as the ten Antibes
landscapes: the artist to have a half-share in the
profits. The real significance of this purchase
lay in the five recent paintings of Giverny: they
would eventually form the core of Monet's second exhibition arranged by Theo in February-
March 1889 (figs. 69, 70).

It seems clear that Alice Hoschedé visited
the exhibition in early March, returning to
Giverny with news of Theo's concern at the
rumour that the artist wished to be released
from his agreement with Boussod and Valadon.
Monet was already thinking of a large retrospective show at the Galerie Georges Petit, together with Roding, to coincide with the 1889
International Exhibition in Paris. He obviously
desired more freedom of action. There was also
the possibility of renewing his relations with
Durand-Ruel. Nevertheless, Monet tried to
allay Theo's fears.

Giverny par Vernon eure

Cher Monsieur Van gogh,
Mme Hoschedé me dit que vous êtes dé-
solé de ce qui est arrivé. Mon dieu j'espère
bien que cela ne nous empêchera pas de
faire des affaires ensemble. Je n'avais du

reste pas demandé la résiliation de notre arrangement, j'avais simplement demandé à Mr Valadon (et cela pour ma sécurité et ma tranquilité au moment de m'absenter) s'il était ou non dans l'intention de rester dans l'exécution du dit arrangement, il me rend mon liberté c'est donc que ces Messieurs ne veulent pas continuer. Nul tort ne vient de moi puisqu'une première fois sur la demande de Mr Boussod fils j'avais consenti à ce qu'il ne prenne qu'un certain nombre des tableaux que j'avais apportés à votre intention. Je serai demain à Paris, devant partir le soir même pour la Creuse. Je serai chez vous entre 11 h½ et midi.

Je voudrai que nous arrangions mon compte avec les nouveaux tableaux vendus et comme j'aurai aussi besoin d'argent, je serai bien aise que sur les cinq tableaux à me prendre vous en choissiseriez deux ou trois parmi ceux qui sont chez vous et le reste à mon retour, cela me ferait plaisir tout en régularisant la situation.

à demain donc
Bien à vous
Claude Monet
5 Mars 89

Monet's visit to Theo on 6 March enabled him to see once again his exhibition, before leaving for a painting campaign in the Creuse, where he stayed until mid-May. The success of the show, marked by a series of highly favourable reviews, especially those of Geffroy and Mirbeau,[17] and by the sale of several pictures, spurred Theo to ask Monet if he would agree to an exhibition of some twenty paintings at the Goupil Gallery in London. Monet consented immediately.

Fresselines 25 Mars (1889)

Cher Monsieur van Gogh
Je veux bien vous confier les tableaux que vous avez à moi pour une exposition à Londres, mais si je suis certain de les avoir pour le 10 mai, et en en exceptant la vue

de Belle-ile que vous avez mise à côté. Quant à vous faire un dessin, je suis si affairé de travail et je n'ai pas sous les yeux la moindre chose à reproduire, tâchez donc de faire pour le mieux comme vous pourrez.

Je voudrais aussi qu'à Londres vous fassiez des prix plus élevés. Veuillez me dire ce que vous pensez faire à ce sujet, et vous répondrai de suite, car il est habituel à Londres de mettre les prix au catalogue.

J'attends donc un mot de vous en même temps vous me direz quels sont les tableaux restant à moi. J'espère que les nouvelles ventes ont à peu près égalisés mon compte, je serai bien aise d'apprendre qu'il se balance à mon avantage.
Recevez mes compliments
Bien à vous
Claude Monet

In mid-April 1889, twenty paintings by Monet went on view at the London branch of Goupil's under the title of 'Impressions by Claude Monet.' The catalogue preface was a translation of Mirbeau's review in *Le Figaro* of 10 March, a review occasioned by Theo's small exhibition in the Boulevard Montmartre. Of the twenty pictures to be seen in London, at least six had been included in the recent Paris show. Theo's part in organising the London show was absolutely crucial, even down to asking Monet for a drawing to reproduce in the catalogue.

Monet wanted his pictures back from London by 10 May for the projected opening of his large retrospective show at Georges Petit's gallery. However, it was not until mid-June that the Petit exhibition eventually opened. Hence, Monet's brief and hastily written note of 7 June concerning the *Paysage avec Figures, Giverny* (W 1024) that Boussod and Valadon were lending to the show.[18]

Hotel du Restaurant de Rome
Garnier
111, Rue St. Lazare
17, Place du Havre
Paris

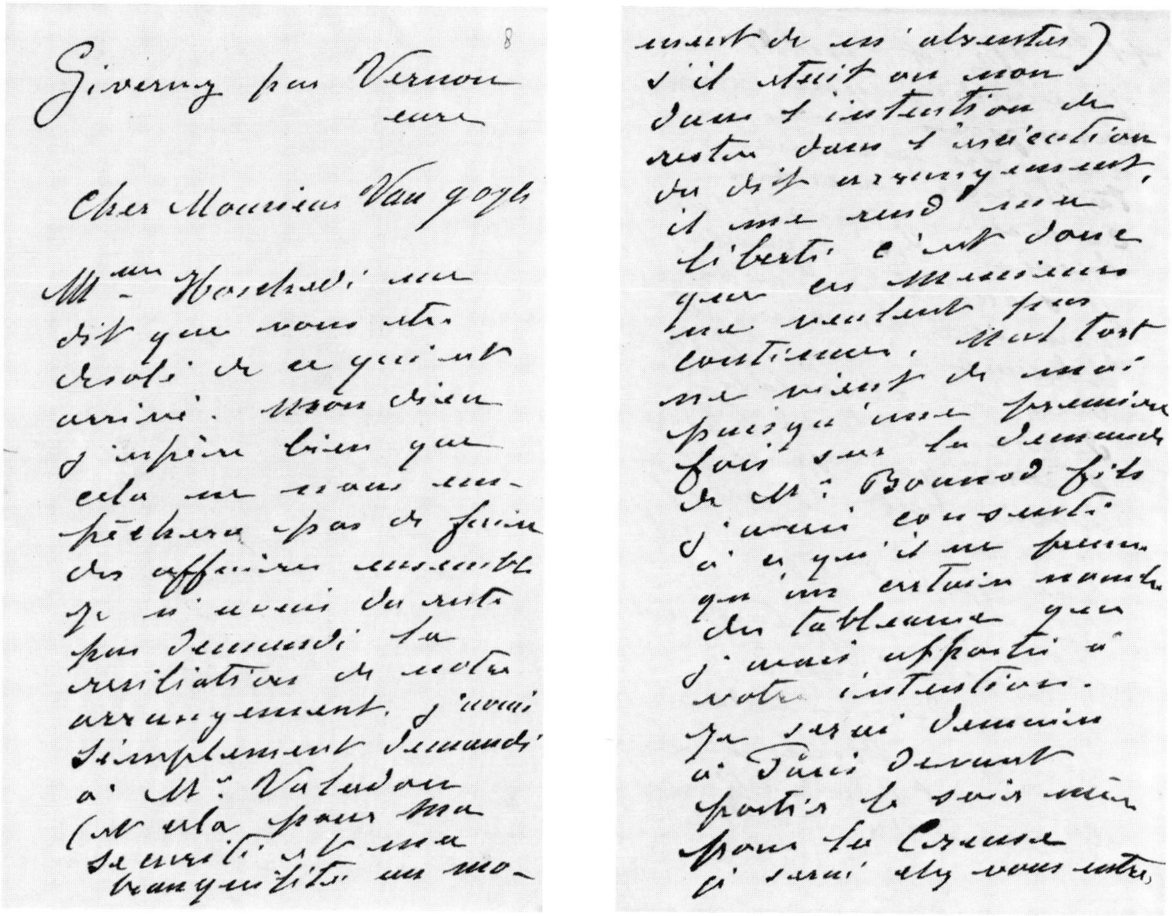

71. Letter of Claude Monet to Theo van Gogh, 5 March 1889.

Cher Monsieur Van gogh,
Je pars dans un moment. Voulez en-
veloper le tableau des figures et le re-
mettre au porteur. M. Faure n'ayant pas
complètement dévernis le sien ne vous l'a
pas envoyé.
Compliments
Claude Monet
7 Juin 89

Two days later, on 9 June, Valadon visited Giverny, probably accompanied by Theo.[19] It must have been on this visit that five more paintings were chosen for purchase. Entered in the stockbook on 20 June, and bought on a cash basis without the artist sharing the profits from sales, these were the last pictures that Theo bought directly from Monet. Between 4 July 1889 and 25 June 1890, he bought a further eighteen paintings by Monet, but all of these came from other dealers, or collectors, or the Paris sale rooms.[20]

There is no evidence of any business contact with Monet during these months; nor of Theo visiting Giverny. But then Monet was engaged almost entirely in organising a subscription to buy Manet's *Olympia* for presentation to the Louvre. From July 1889 to Spring 1890, his energies were spent in writing to artists, critics and collectors, and in lobbying politicians and bureaucrats. He scarcely put brush to canvas during this period.

However, he must have met Theo on one occasion in Paris, sometime between 19 March and 27 April. For Monet certainly visited the exhibition of the Salon des Indépendants, where ten paintings by Vincent van Gogh were hung. According to Theo's letter to his brother of 23 April 1890: 'Monet said that your pictures were the best of all in the exhibition.'[21]

The next clue to any contact between Theo and Monet also occurs in a letter from Theo to Vincent. On 5 July 1890, he wrote: 'I have reserved the day of 14 July to go and see Claude Monet along with Valadon, who will be sure to annoy me that day, but I am glad I am going to see new pictures by Monet.'[22]

Hitherto, there has been speculation as to

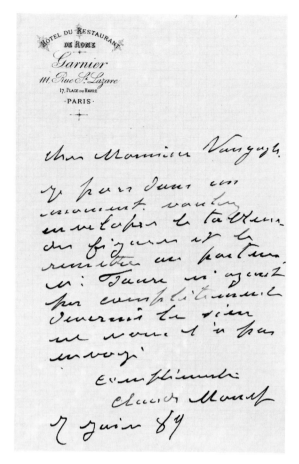

72. Letter of Claude Monet to Theo van Gogh, 7 June 1889.

Ruel m'ayant acheté un certain nombre. Je vous préviendrai quand j'aurai des choses intéressantes à vous montrer, si le temps se remet au beau, ce sera plus tôt que je pense.
recevez mes compliments
cordialement à vous Claude Monet

J'ai eu ces jours-ci la visite de Mr. La Rochefoucauld qui m'a dit vous avoir acheté le pin au bord de la Méditerranée, ce qui m'a fait plaisir, c'en est ceci un au moins qui a chance de ne pas aller en Amérique.[23]
C.M.

A further reason, not mentioned by Monet, was that his friends Mallarmé and Berthe Morisot planned to visit him on 14 July.[24] In the event, Theo left Paris on Bastille Day with Jo and their baby, bound for Leiden where his mother would see her grandson for the first time.[25]

By the end of July, Theo's happiness was transformed into the profoundest sorrow. Vincent's death left him inconsolable. He told his mother on 1 August: 'Life was such a burden to him; but now, as often happens, everybody is full of praise for his talents.'[26] Monet's letter of condolence was written two weeks later.

why Theo did not visit Monet as planned. Monet's letter of 10 July explains:

Giverny par Vernon eure
10 Juillet 90

Cher Monsieur Van Gogh,
Je n'ai pas répondu de suite à votre lettre parce que je n'étais pas certain d'être ici le 14 juillet et que j'attendais d'être fixé moi-même pour vous en prévenir.
Donc si vous voulez en prévenir Mr. Valadon, je vous demande d'ajourner votre visite au mois d'août, cela viendra mieux sous tous les rapports car avec l'épouvantable temps que nous avons le travail va mal et je tiens à vous montrer autre chose que des essais inachevés. Avec cela je suis un peu à court de tableaux. Mr. Durand-

Giverny par Vernon eure
15 Août 90

Cher Monsieur Van Gogh
Je vous prie de m'excuser. Je voulais chaque jour vous adresser un mot de condoléances pour le malheur qui vous a frappé mais je suis dans une telle crise de travail je suis dehors depuis 4 hrs du matin et ne rentrant que pour les repas et si absorbé que j'oublie tout le reste.
Vous voudrez bien m'excuser n'est-ce pas et croire combien j'ai été touché pour vous d'une telle perte. Je vous ai dit ce que je pensais de votre frère, c'est un double malheur pour vous.
Recevez mes meilleurs compliments
et croyez moi
tout à vous
Claude Monet

90

Monet and Theo must have had one last meeting in late September 1890, when they discussed the intentions of Boussod and Valadon ('ces messieurs') regarding Monet's future with them. Durand-Ruel was very much back in favour by now, having recently bought ten paintings. Yet there was still the possibility of Theo and Valadon visiting Giverny also to select some recent paintings. Monet wrote his last letter to Theo on 7 October 1890, two days before Theo's breakdown.

Giverny par Vernon eure
7 Oct 90

Cher Monsieur Van Gogh,
Je serai bien aise de savoir si vous avez fait part de notre conversation à ces Messieurs et quelles sont leurs intentions. Je voudrais bien terminer mon compte et arriver à une entente au sujet des quelques tableaux qui vous restent et auxquels je suis intéressés.
Vous serez bien aimable de m'écrire un mot à ce sujet. Comme je vous l'ai dit, j'ai eu la visite de Monsieur Durand-Ruel qui m'a acheté une dizaine de toiles de différentes époques dont quatre de cette année. Si donc Mr. Valadon se décidait à venir avec vous vous pourrez voir pas mal de choses nouvelles d'autant que je suis en pleine veine de travail en ce moment. En tous cas faites moi part des intentions de ces messieurs. J'espère qu'avec ce beau temps vous aurez pu vous remettre de votre indisposition.
Bien à vous
Claude Monet

The letters of Theo van Gogh to Johanna Bonger

Besides the letters of Monet to Theo, Theo's letters to his fiancée Johanna Borger contain valuable information. Apart from their inherent fascination as first-hand confessions, with all the unrehearsed immediacy of a private letter, these letters considerably extend our knowledge of the second exhibition that Theo gave Monet. The following extracts from these letters, which belong to the Vincent van Gogh Foundation, are here published for the first time.

6 February 1889

Tomorrow my exhibition of the latest works by Monet will be opened, so I'm uncommonly busy, but more of this later (...)
As I told you I am busy organising an exhibition, of Monet mainly, but in addition I shall show some pastels by Degas and a marble statue by Rodin.[27] All other paintings have been put away & it looks very beautiful upstairs with those chosen works of art and nothing inferior. Tomorrow the journalists and some acquaintances are invited, and during the following fortnight several hundreds of people have been asked to come.
It is gratifying now and then because sometimes there are people who do take such great pleasure in it. Of course those with whom I have most dealings, the buyers, are not the most interesting of the visitors, but if I sell well this time I shall be double pleased, in the circumstances. One sees hardly any paintings by Monet in the city, so there is a chance of its being a success. As soon as I can I shall write to you of the paintings themselves; this letter has to be sent now.

9 February 1889

There is a contrast between this work of art (by Rodin) and Monet's paintings in so far as where Rodin moves the souls of the spectators by arousing thoughts of what death is, Monet does the same by telling about life.[28] His trees are freshly grown and their foliage is thick, the wind makes the branches rustle and the leaves quiver, the (leaves of the) poplars turn in the breeze so that their grey backs lit by the sun diffuse a silvery haze over the trees. A river with its clear stream of water at the foot of the trees, the clear blue sky above, it all breathes freshness and health. Another time it is a large stretch of pasture bordered in the distance by hills and trees, at dusk at the moment when just before it vanishes the sun spreads out its golden beams so gloriously over everything. The shadows are long and the young people approaching us across the pasture in a group are seen against the light. In front a young girl dressed in a pink frock, straw hat and her hair hanging loose. Between two petits diables de frères, in light blue suits, further on a young couple, everything bathed in a blaze of sun & light, for although one sees the figures against the sun they are also lit in front by the strong reflection of the light on the grassland (fig. 70).

Then again it is the chain of rocks along the shore of the Mediterranean which is unvaryingly washed by the water in its ceaseless motion. Again it is in the full sun in the foreground, the water multi-coloured from the glittering light on the uneven surface of the little waves, gradually it turns a deep blue, broken in places by the violet shadow of a cloud, in the far distance a deep green against the horizon so that one rather sees the snowy tops of the Alps red in contrast. On top of the rocks, to the left, a lone little white custom-house stands out against the blue sky. In all the paintings on show there is light and life, often glaring sunlight and each picture gives rise to the same sensation that nature itself would have brought about. As far as colour is concerned there is a richness in it.

As with the painting in the window at Tersteeg's, which reminded me of a shower of lapis-lazuli, here too one's thoughts are often turned to precious stones, mother-of-pearl, crystal or silver. The very lines have a grace which makes one think of something precious. Although Monet is not so radical as Degas & other geniuses, he has in any case the gift of being able to cast a ray of light in these pessimistic times, one that will bring clarity and encouragement to many.

11 February 1889

Fortunately I am busy with the Monet exhibition. If the weather were better more people would come but those who defy the gales and snow to come and see them are the least indifferent, and there is a greater opportunity for discussion, for once. Among the visitors there are many men of letters, and although they cannot always make a just assessment, at all events they do their best. For the moment I cannot wish for more since I have already sold some.

13 Febuary 1889

The weather here is such as to discourage the most cheerful of men. Alternately rain and snow, freezing cold one day and mild the next. Surely this is keeping people away from the Monet exhibition, for apart from some enthusiasts there are not many visitors. It is true that the main purpose of the exhibition is to oblige congenial spirits, but after the articles on it in the newpapers they should be clamouring at the doors. Nothing good has been said about it yet, other than the usual newspaper compliments, otherwise I would have sent you something, but something is bound to come.

22 February 1889

The exhibition is quite a success, although many more spectators than buyers.

11 March 1889

My dearest Jo, this evening I am sending you a copy of the Figaro containing an article on the Monet paintings. It gave me a great deal of pleasure and caused quite a sensation here. At first the Figaro did not want to include it since it is very much at odds with the usual sentiments of the newspaper, but when Mirbeau threatened to resign on account of it, it was printed after all.

This afternoon people were flocking to the gallery and it is as if since yesterday Monet has become a great artist, which he has been for so long. I am very pleased about it and just wanted to tell you this.

Did you receive the other day that article from the 'Justice' I sent you? I thought it a better article as such but this one will be more influential since it is in the Figaro. Sooner or later it will have to be admitted that this new movement offers something firm to go by.

14 March 1889

People are thronging the gallery to see the exhibition and moreover I have to act as cashier since the bookkeeper is ill; in the evenings I am so tired that I cannot bring myself to write.

Giverny par Vernon
Eure
15 Aout 90

Cher Monsieur Van Gogh,
je vous prie de m'excuser. Je voulais chaque jour vous adresser un mot de condoléance pour le malheur qui vous a frappé mais je suis dans une telle crise de travail. Je suis dehors depuis 5 h. du matin et ne rentrant que pour les repas. Et si absorbé que j'oublie tout le reste. Vous voudrez bien m'excuser et croire combien j'ai été touché pour vous d'une telle perte. Je vous ai dit ce que je pensais de votre frère, c'est un double malheur pour vous.
Recevez mes meilleurs compliments et croyez moi
tout à vous
Claude Monet.

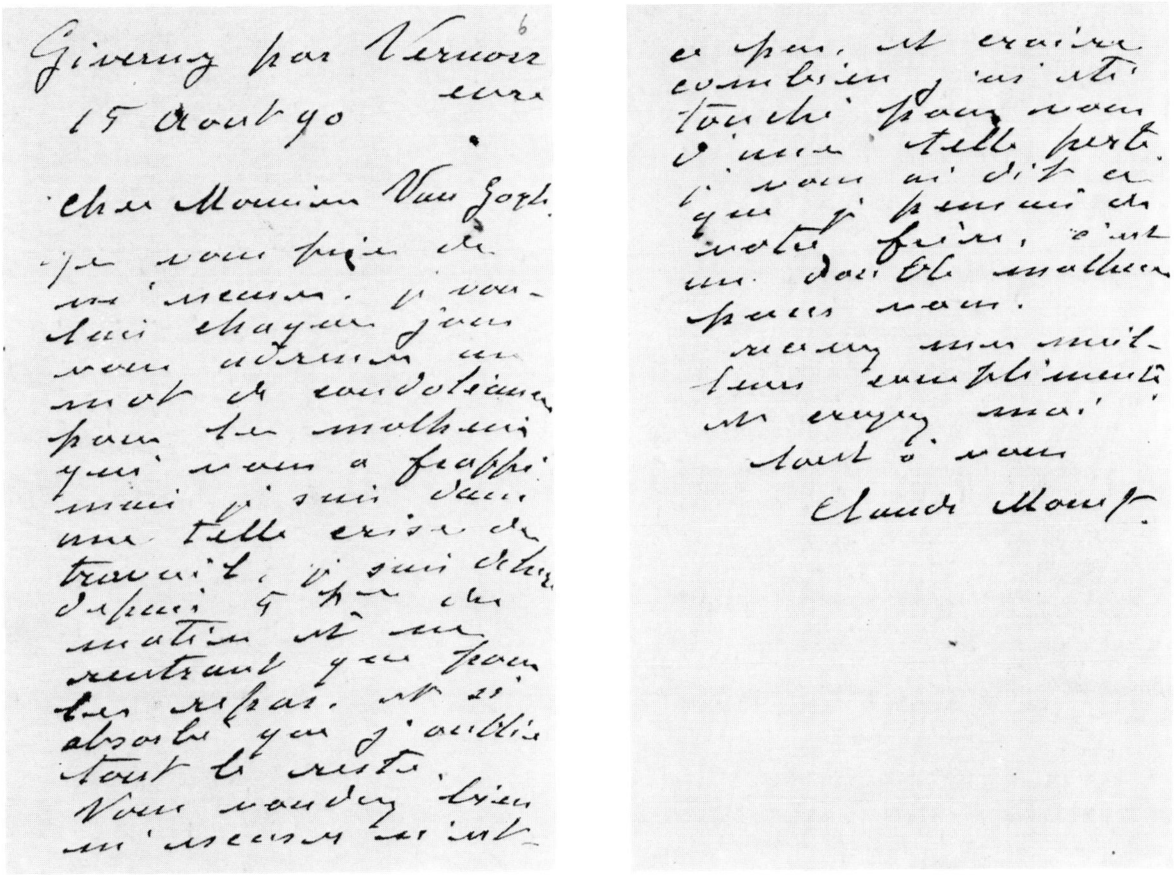

73. Letter of Claude Monet to Theo van Gogh, 15 August 1890.

18 March 1889

For curiosity's sake I am sending you a note from Mirbeau which I received from him and which makes it clear why he gave an effusion of enthusiasm rather than a review. Magnard is the managing editor and Wolff the art critic of the Figaro.

Conclusions

These extracts help clarify the following:
1. The exhibition opened on 7 February 1889, much earlier than was previously realised – perhaps because reviews did not appear in the daily press until the beginning of March. It probably remained on view until 30 March, when Theo left Paris for Holland and his forthcoming marriage on 18 April. And in any case, the paintings had to be sent to London for Monet's show at the Goupil Gallery in mid-April.
2. There was no catalogue. But one noteworthy phenomenon – perhaps common practice in the 1880s? – was the sending of special invitations to 'hundreds of people' to visit the exhibition during the first two weeks, an extended private view, as it were.
3. The exhibition was made up predominantly of Monet's recent works: that is, autumn landscapes and figure-paintings executed in Giverny, five of which Theo had purchased on 31 December 1888. In addition, Theo described to Jo an Antibes painting; while Geffroy in *La Justice* described a painting of *Meules* (W 1213), a view of Vétheuil (W 518), and a still life of chrysanthemums (W 1212). In all, there were probably ten paintings on view.

74. Letter of Claude Monet to Theo van Gogh, 7 October 1890.

4. Theo displayed, in addition to Monet's canvases, a marble sculpture by Rodin, and some Degas pastels.

5. During the period from 6 February to 30 March 1889, Theo sold five paintings by Monet. Three were of Antibes (sold on 6 February, 16 March and 27 March); the others belonged to the recently completed Giverny paintings – *Les Meules* (sold on 26 February) and a *Prairie de Limetz* (sold on 12 March). During the showing of Monet's ten Antibes landscapes in June 1888, Theo had also sold five paintings. If a commercial justification were needed for these exhibitions, then Boussod and Valadon could hardly complain of such results.

6. The critical responses, especially those of Gustave Geffroy and Octave Mirbeau, were of cardinal importance in furthering Monet's reputation in Paris. The effect of a newspaper review – particularly one on the front page of *Le Figaro* – was, as Theo noted, instant and widespread.

* For Johan and Anneke van Gogh. Monet's paintings are mentioned by their catalogue number in Wildenstein's *catalogue raisonné*. English translations of Monet's letters are given in Appendix IV.

1. John Rewald, 'Theo van Gogh, Goupil and the Impressionists', *Gazette des Beaux-Arts* 8 (1973), pp. 1-108. See also: Lili Jampoller, 'Theo van Gogh and Camille Pissarro: correspondence and an exhibition', *Simiolus* 16 (1986), pp. 50-61.

2. These figures are based on the lists established by Rewald, *op. cit.* (note 1), pp. 89-104.

3. Both were sold to Henri Poidatz, director of *Le Matin*. One of them (W 1091) was included in Poidatz's sale, Hôtel Drouot, Paris, 15 March 1888, lot 62, where it was bought back by Theo van Gogh.

4. The Degas pastel over monotype, *La Femme à la Toilette*; P.A. Lemoisne, *Degas et son oeuvre*, 4 vols., Paris 1946-49, vol. 3, no. 890.

5. Daniel Wildenstein, *Claude Monet: Biographie et catalogue raisonné*, 4 vols., Lausanne & Paris, 1974-85, vol. 3, letter 784.
6. See Rewald, op. cit. (note 1), pp. 98-99.
7. Wildenstein, op. cit. (note 5), vol. 3, letter 799.
8. *Village de Bennecourt* was entered in the stockbook as bought from Monet on 21 April 1888. See Rewald, op. cit. (note 1), p. 99.
9. Van Gogh to Theo, *The complete letters of Vincent van Gogh*, 3 vols., London 1958, vol. 2, p. 561; letter 483 of *circa* 7 May 1888.
10. Rewald, op. cit. (note 1), p. 23.
11. Wildenstein, op. cit. (note 5), vol. 3, letter 903.
12. Gustave Geffroy's article was later reprinted in his book, *La Vie Artistique*, Paris 1894, pp. 77-81.
13. Van Gogh to Theo, *Complete Letters*, cit. (note 9), vol. 3, p. 590, Letter 501 of *circa* 21 June 1888.
14. Letter 1425; *circa* 20 June 1888, Wildenstein, vol. 3.
15. Letter 906 of 1 October 1888 to an unknown recipient; Wildenstein, op. cit. (note 5), vol. 3.
16. Rewald, op. cit. (note 1), pp. 99-100.
17. Gustave Geffroy in *La Justice* of 5 March 1889, later reprinted in his book *La Vie Artistique*, Paris 1894, pp. 81-87; and Octave Mirbeau in *Le Figaro* of 10 March 1889.
18. This painting was included by Theo in his small Monet exhibition of February-March 1889, having been one of the five Giverny paintings bought from Monet on 31 December 1888. It was also shown in Monet's exhibition at the Goupil Gallery, London, in April-May 1889, as '*X. Prairie and Figures.*' For Theo's description of this painting see his letter of 9 February 1889 to Johanna Bonger.
19. Valadon's visit to Giverny on 9 June 1889 was referred to by Monet in his letter of 10 June to Hamman (Letter 989, Wildenstein, op. cit. (note 5), vol. 3.). Monet did not mention Theo in his letter.
20. Rewald, op. cit. (note 1), pp. 100-101.
21. Theo's letter to Vincent of 23 April 1890, *Complete letters*, cit. (note 9), vol. 3, p. 568.
22. Theo's letter to Vincent of 5 July 1890, *Complete letters*, cit. (note 9), vol. 3, p. 567.
23. Comte de la Rochefoucauld bought the painting from Theo on 25 May 1890. See Rewald, op. cit. (note 1), p. 101.
24. See Monet's letters to Mallarmé and Berthe Morisot, both of 11 July 1890. Letters 1064 and 1065 in Wildenstein, op. cit. (note 5), vol. 3.
25. See Theo's letter to Vincent, dated 14 July 1890, *Complete letters*, cit. (note 9), vol. 3, p. 577.
26. See J. van Gogh-Bonger, 'Memoir of Vincent van Gogh', *Complete letters*, cit. (note 9), vol. 1, p. LIII.
27. This statue of Rodin was a marble head of St. John the Baptist on a plate, as is clear from Theo's letter of 9 February.
28. See note 27.

CATALOGUE

Ronald Pickvance

Topographical information

Boudewijn Bakker & Marijke de Groot

Titles

Titles for individual paintings are variously giv-ven in dealer's stockbook, Monet's account-book, and exhibition catalogues. Some examples of the variations are given in the catalogue entries. In all three sections of the catalogue – Zaandam, Amsterdam and the Bulb Fields – the titles are given as precisely as possible in terms of the topographical location. Topographical research on the Zaandam period can be found in the publications of F. Mars; see the bibliography. Additional topographical information has been given by J.D. Bakker and J.P. Vooren. The Bulb Fields have been located by M. Hulkenberg, S.C.H. Leenheer and E. van de Wetering.

Provenance and Exhibitions

Full detail of previous owners of each painting or of previous exhibitions are not given. They can be found in Daniel Wildenstein, *Claude Monet: Biographie et catalogue raisonné*, 4 vols., Lausanne & Paris 1974-85. Some allusions, however, are made to important early collectors of Monet's paintings; and to their inclusion in exhibitions in the 1870s and 1880s.

Reference to the Literature

These are confined to the citation of the relevant catalogue number in Wildenstein, *op. cit.,* abbreviated to W.

MAP OF THE ZAANDAM REGION

The numbers refer to the catalogue entries.

98

ZAANDAM

Claude Monet lived in Zaandam for four months: from early June to 8 October 1871. In the only two letters to survive from his stay, both written to Camille Pissarro in June, he gave his address as the Hotel de Beurs, where he and his family were 'très bien installés', and said they would remain in Zaandam for the summer. It is assumed that Monet, his wife Camille (1847-79) and their son Jean (born August 1867) continued to live at the Hotel de Beurs throughout their stay; and that Camille gave French conversation lessons, especially to the wealthy Van de Stadt family who lived on the Zuiddijk, to help support them. Monet presumably managed to live in Zaandam without financial worries despite the fact that he evidently did not sell any of his pictures. But the death of his father in January 1871 had provided a small inheritance. On the other hand, there is no evidence that he was supported by the great Paris dealer, Paul Durand-Ruel (1830-1922), whom he had met in London during his stay there in the winter of 1870-71. It was not until April 1872 – more than four months after Monet's return to Paris – that Durand-Ruel bought a Zaandam painting from the artist; and only in May 1872 that he bought three others.

Little is known of Monet's life or Dutch connections in Zaandam. How he became acquainted with the Van de Stadt family remains a mystery. But once acquainted, the Van de Stadts may have introduced him to other wealthy families living on the west of the Zaan (see especially cat. nos. 6-8). More certain is the fact that Monet met – for the first time – Henry Havard (1838-1921), French art critic, historian and travel writer, who had been forced into exile because of his participation in the Commune as a 'commandant' of the National Guard, and whose passport had been issued in Lille on 27 May 1871, one day before the collapse of the Commune. As well as Havard, Monet told Pissarro on 17 June that he had just met the French painter Henri Michel-Lévy (1844-1914), 'who must spend some time here as well'.

Havard and Michel-Lévy also stayed at the Hotel de Beurs. On 26 June, it was reported that Monet, Havard and Michel-Lévy often walked and rowed on the Zaan, and that 'the two artists were seen working from time to time'. Havard left Zaandam sometime in July; Michel-Lévy by the end of July. According to the police report, Monet was the only Frenchman left.

The three compatriots visited the Trippenhuis collection in Amsterdam on 22 June. Other French artists to visit the Trippenhuis during the summer of 1871 included Carolus-Duran (21 June), Antoine Vollon (24 July), Jules Jacquemart (6 September), and Charles-François Daubigny and his artist-son Karl (18 September). Of these, Carolus-Duran had been a friend of Monet's in the 1860's, and had painted his portrait in 1867 (now Musée Marmottan, Paris); while Daubigny had supported Monet's submissions to the Salon jury, and more recently introduced him to Durand-Ruel in London. Yet there is no evidence that Monet met them in Holland. He must indeed have been the lone Frenchman working in Zaandam in August and September 1871.

Police records show that Monet finally left Zaandam for Amsterdam on 8 October 1871. It seems unlikely that he stayed very long: not long enough, in any case, to paint any pictures. It was about 10 October that he signed the visitors' book of the Frans Hals Museum at Haarlem. Most probably he returned to Paris soon afterwards, although his first surviving letter from there – again to Camille Pissarro – was not written until 19 November.

During his four months' stay in Zaandam, Monet produced some twenty-five paintings. He found the town very agreeable, telling Pissarro on 2 June: 'Zaandam is particularly remarkable and there is enough to paint there for a lifetime.' By 17 June, he was more explicit: 'It is marvellous for painting here; there is everything you can find "de plus amusant". Houses of all colours, hundreds of windmills and ravishing boats (...) and with all this very fine weather, so that already I have several canvases on the go.'

Already, the various motifs that would attract him throughout his stay were announced – houses, windmills and boats. Yet it is difficult to determine a convincing chronological sequence. Only two paintings are dated 1871: the

Portrait of Guurtje van de Stadt (cat. no. 25) and the small, picturesque corner of Zaandam that Monet gave to Henry Havard (cat. no. 19). Two other paintings are dated 1872 (cat. nos. 6 and 20), but these seem to have been dated when Monet sold them, and cannot be used as evidence that he returned to Holland in 1872.

To suggest a chronological sequence for the twenty-four landscapes catalogued here would be hazardous. There are no marked seasonal changes from June to October: for instance, clear signs of early autumn colours in Monet's treatment of the foliage that would suggest a September-October dating. Nor can the traditional custom of changing the windmill sails after 30 September, from their summer red and white to their winter yellow and brown, help very much, since Monet stayed in Zaandam for one week only after the change. There is no late windmill painting.

On the assumption that Monet's wife, Camille, appears in some five paintings (cat. nos. 6, 7, 8, 9, 15), her various dresses, hats and parasols (she was especially fashion-conscious) provide no clue to the dating of her husband's pictures.

The motifs of all but three of these two dozen landscapes can be located with certainty. And in the case of the three exceptions, a general location can be suggested (cat. nos. 13, 14 and 19). Monet's mobility in his selection of motifs can be followed on the map. In cataloguing the Zaandam paintings, it has been thought best to arrange them in topographical groupings.

1. The harbour near the Dam and its immediate vicinity (cat. nos. 1-5).

2. The Achterzaan: views on the Zaan river running north from the Dam, and including one view of a canal that runs east from the Zaan (cat. nos. 6-12).

3. Views to the west of Zaandam; two of canals in the Westzijderveld (cat. nos. 13, 14), one looking west on the Hogendijk (cat. no. 15).

4. Views to the south-east of the harbour (cat. nos. 16-24), which include a pic-

turesque corner of Zaandam off the Zuiddijk (cat. no. 19), a view of the Weerpad (cat. no. 23), and Monet's most southern motif, leading to the IJ (cat. no. 24).

5. Finally, the only figure-painting Monet executed in Zaandam, the *Portrait of Guurtje van de Stadt* (cat. no. 25).

These clusters of works do not imply that Monet worked systematically in one area before moving to the next: for instance, that he deliberately moved northwards up the Zaan stage by stage. In brief, no chronological progression is implied in this guided tour of Zaandam.

It seems doubtful that a definitive stylistic progression could be proposed. Nevertheless, some deductions can be made about Monet's working procedures and his painterly intentions. None of his Zaandam paintings can be called large. His favorite format was on canvas of standard French size, 48 x 73 cm. Nine paintings have this size. Some nine others are painted on a narrower, more horizontal format, with slight variations in their dimensions, some of which approach a double-square shape. There are four exceptions to these two major types: the portrait (which in effect simply converts a horizontal into a vertical canvas); two landscapes of squarer format (cat. nos. 8 and 15), and the only upright landscape (cat. no. 19).

Monet sometimes produced a contrasting pair of paintings, in which changes both in weather and time of day were conveyed by marked variations in handling and colour. Two such pairs overtly demonstrate this: two views of windmills and water (cat. nos. 20 and 21), and two of canals with footbridges (cat. nos. 13 and 14). In each pair, a day effect, with wind rippling the water, is contrasted with an evening sunset, calm and still.

A different kind of contrast can be seen in cat. nos. 11 and 12. While the same stretch of the Zaan with its windmills is shown, the variations are dictated much more by Monet's choice and intention. In the one (cat. no. 11), the composition is more studied and slightly *retardataire*, as though he were painting a homage to Jongkind: there is subdued sunshine, from which Monet succeeds in conveying a subtle and evocative symphony in red. In the other (cat. no. 12), he selected a horizontal canvas, 'sliced' the boats and mooring-post in the left foreground giving a sense of informal immediacy, and observed the scene in grey weather making his colour scheme more tonal.

It is only rarely – at least in those paintings that survive from the 1860s and 1870s – that a working process can be seen that involves a small, very rapid sketch done on the spot *(pochade)*, and a worked-up painting deriving from it. And there is no such clear-cut distinction in Monet's paintings from Zaandam. The nearest he came to it is in the three related views of the Voorzaan (see cat. nos. 16-18).

There is, however, one painting that is more finished than the others, and also much more deliberately composed. In *The Mill 'Het Oosterkattegat'* (cat. no. 22), Monet has carefully plotted his composition, so that the planes succeed each other clearly and recession is marked out for the viewer. In the massing of windmill and fishing boat as a main focus of interest, Monet seems again to be conscious of Jongkind.

He worked with great rapidity in other paintings, and almost certainly without later retouching (e.g. cat. no. 18). And yet others – surprisingly, given their evident spontaneity – show changes of mind made during the actual execution: a windmill painted out of one (cat. no. 12) or a sail out of another (cat. no. 21).

When Eugène Boudin (1824-98) saw Monet's Zaandam paintings in January 1872, he wrote to a friend: 'He has brought some very beautiful studies from Holland and I believe that he is meant to take one of the leading places in our school.'

In fact, Monet had brought back to Paris twenty-three landscapes. Within his artistic development, the Zaandam paintings are often seen as a connecting link, a stylistic bridge, between his studies of the Seine at la Grenouillère in 1869 and his long continuation of such studies at Argenteuil, in the northern suburbs of Paris, between 1872 and 1877. Yet they have their own authentic voice. Monet captures the Dutchness, not merely externally – of fishing boat and windmill, town house and *luchthuis*, river and canal – but also the delicate enveloping light and atmosphere, subtly different from the luminosity of the Ile de France. The superb manner in which he registers the immense and often changing Dutch skies is sufficient proof of this.

Boudin knew Monet's work well, from the late 1850s onward: his words were high praise indeed – and acutely prophetic. (And Monet's views of Holland may have tempted Boudin himself to make his first visit there in 1873.) Historically, the Zaandam paintings constitute the first large group of Monet's work from one place and one continuous campaign. (From his eight-month stay in London in 1870-71 – twice as long as his stay in Zaandam – only six paintings survive, and it is unlikely that many are lost or destroyed.) They launch the increasingly productive Monet of the 1870s, who usually worked on medium-sized canvases, characterised by informal compositions, fluidity of handling, and unity of vision.

A selected few – three or four, no more – were often illustrated and discussed in early monographs and histories of Impressionism. It was not until 1974 with the publication of Daniel Wildenstein's *catalogue raisonné* that the entire body of Monet's Zaandam oeuvre was brought together. They have never been exhibited together – and given the difficulties of locating the present whereabouts of some, and of persuading owners to lend others, it is doubtful that they ever will. Monet himself chose three for his first one-man show at Durand-Ruel's gallery in March 1883 (see cat. nos. 11, 15, 20). Two of these (cat. nos. 11 and 20) he selected once again for his large retrospective show at the Georges Petit gallery in 1889: the third one chosen for this occasion – 'Canal; Zaandam, 1871' belonging to M. Leclanché – cannot now be identified with certainty. For Monet, cat. nos. 11 and 20 were plainly seen as his most important *exhibition pictures*: Daubigny had chosen one for his own collection, and Faure, a successful operatic baritone, had chosen the other.

Not many French artists followed Monet's lead and worked in Zaandam. The few paintings

Maxime Lalanne, *Zaandam.* From: Henry Havard, *La Hollande à vol d'oiseau,* Paris 1881.

Henri Michel-Lévy might have done during his six-week stay in June-July 1871 have not come down to us. French artists visiting Holland later – whether Boudin in 1873 and again in 1884 or Signac in 1906 – ignored Zaandam. Lalanne, however, did visit this town in the 1870s, probably in the company of Havard, whose book *La Hollande à vol d'oiseau* of 1881 was illustrated by the artist. Only Guillaumin went, in 1904, to Zaandam on the advice of Monet (G. Serret and D. Fabiani, *Armand Guillaumin 1841-1927,*

Paris, not dated, p. 74).

More than a century after Monet's sojourn there, much has changed in the town. Most of the eastern bank of the Zaan has been taken over by factories; much of the colour has disappeared from the domestic architecture; there are few windmills left, the fishing fleet has gone, and the harbour has been rebuilt. For the evocation of 'old' Zaandam, the Dutch paintings of Claude Monet become invaluable historical documents.

Jean-Baptiste Armand Guillaumin, *Zaandam*. The Hague, Art Gallery Ivo Bouwman B.V.

1 THE HARBOUR AND THE DAM

Oil on canvas, 47 x 74 cm
Signed lower left: Claude Monet
W 188
Private collection

The view shows the west side of the harbour, with the boats moored the length of the Hogendijk, and in the background the houses of the Damstraat. Monet took his vantage-point from the landing-stage of the society Trouw en Verbintenis, part of whose building is visible at the far left.

Monet painted four views of the Dam (cat. nos. 1-4) which was easily reached from the Hotel De Beurs. These were probably among the first works he did in Zaandam. With his inborn fascination for boats and water, Monet would have been inevitably drawn to the harbour and reminded of similar scenes he had painted in Honfleur, Fécamp, and to a lesser degree, Trouville, between 1866 and 1870 (W 75-77, 116-119, 154).

This atmospheric evocation of a fading sunset, the sky streaked with yellows and pinks, has pictorial affinities with such Barbizon artists as Rousseau and Daubigny. But the bold abbreviated treatment and compositional licence are entirely Monet's own. His honest acceptance of the wooden mooring-post as an enlarged foreground element would have shocked conservative critics of the 1870s. They

would have condemned it as an ugly intrusion, antipicturesque, throwing out the scale and recession, like the enlarged scroll of a cello in a Degas theatre scene. Such out-of-scale and obtrusive foreground objects characterized Japanese woodblock prints.

The firm linear silhouette, seen in *contrejour*, of the mooring-post, contrasts with its reflection in the water, rapidly conveyed in the continuous corkscrew-like brushstrokes. Reflections elsewhere are rendered by a series of bold horizontal, or brickshaped strokes. These shorthand conventions for defining reflections on water were first fully exploited by Monet in his paintings of La Grenouillère, a boating and bathing establishment on the Seine outside Paris. There, in the summer of 1869, he explored several alternative compositions (W 134-136). And in some of the Zaandam paintings, a similar combination of corkscrew (or wriggle) and brick-shaped strokes often recur. (Henceforth referred to as 'wriggle' and 'brick' strokes.)

Monet used his sketchbook to note *motifs*, rather than to make a specific preliminary drawing for a painting. Such a drawing exists of this motif (fig. 1), where Monet got closer to the

1. Claude Monet, *The harbour and the Dam*. Paris, Musée Marmottan.

mooring-post, probably by sitting in a boat (Musée Marmottan sketchbook, inv. 5128, folio 31 verso).

The early history of the painting is unclear. It was with Durand-Ruel by 1888; by 1903 it was with the German dealer Paul Cassirer in Berlin. Monet's friend Théodore Duret (1838-1927), art critic, collector (see cat. no. 11) and first historian of the Impressionists, illustrated it in the 1906 edition of his book, *Histoire des Peintres Impressionnistes*.

2 THE HARBOUR AND THE DAM

Oil on canvas, 45 x 72 cm
Signed lower left: Claude Monet
W 189
Private collection

As in cat. no. 1, the view shows the west side of the harbour, with boats moored alongside the Hogendijk, and in the background a few houses in the Damstraat. At the left, more of the buildings of the Society Trouw en Verbintenis is visible. Monet has moved further in, dispensed with the foreground repoussoir of the mooring-post, and concentrated on a closer-up view of the boats in harbour. Again it recalls some of the harbour scenes painted on the Normandy coast at Honfleur and Le Havre (see especially W 75, 76, 116).

A photograph of the same motif exists, taken approximately at the same time (fig. 2).

Unfortunately, the painting is known to us only from a black-and-white photograph, which makes its particular qualities of light and colour difficult to assess. But Monet has clearly depicted a different time of day to that in cat. no. 1: late morning as against evening.

When Durand-Ruel acquired the picture is not documented, but in 1882, he sold it to the banker, Ernest May (1845-1923) who was then building up a considerable collection of Impressionist works that included several important

Monets. Some of these were sold in Paris on 4 June 1890, among them the present painting which was re-acquired by Durand-Ruel. Never exhibited, nor discussed in any writings on Monet, *The Harbour and the Dam* must be one of his finest Zaandam paintings, *la peinture claire* at its most expressive.

2. *The harbour and the Dam*, c. 1870-1880. Photo: Zaandam, Municipal Archives Zaanstad.

3 THE HARBOUR AND THE DAM

Oil on canvas, 44.5 x 72.5 cm
Signed lower left: Claude Monet
W 190
Private collection

Taken from the vicinity of Hotel de Beurs, looking north-west, this view shows the houses of the Hogendam on the right and in the centre the customs houses and the Grote Sluis.

A photograph, taken a few years after Monet's stay in Zaandam, is very close to the motif of the painting, with only a slight variation in viewpoint (fig. 3).

As in cat. no. 1, Monet has observed the dramatic effects of sunset, with his distinctive 'wriggle' and 'brick' strokes vividly registering the dazzle and reflections on the water. The lurid sky, however, has a striking coloration: instead of streaks of pinks and yellows, mottled patches of grey-violet and yellow-greens pick up the meshed reflections of the water. The painting demonstrates Monet's unerring command of *contre-jour:* structure is not sacrificed in striving to capture sunset effects on the building.

The early history of the painting is unclear. It may be the one entered in Monet's *carnet de comptes* as *Coucher de Soleil, Hollande,* sold to the artist's colourman and small art dealer, Louis Latouche in 1872. Like cat. no. 2, this painting was never exhibited in Monet's lifetime.

108

3. *The harbour and the Dam*, c. 1870-1880. Photo: Zaandam, Municipal Archives Zaanstad.

4 THE DAM AND THE LOCKS ON THE ACHTERZAAN

Oil on canvas, 44 x 72.5 cm
Signed lower left: Claude Monet
W 191
United States, private collection

Monet has here focused on the north side of the small and large locks seen from the Achterzaan in a south-east direction. It is probably painted from a boat. The building to the far right, Dam 2, still exists: it was the Freemasons lodge, Anna Paulowna. The still existing customs houses can be seen in the background (fig. 6).

From Monet's vantage-point and the fall of the shadows on the roof of the central house, *The Dam on the Achterzaan* seems to be a late morning evocation – like cat. no. 2. It is probably the most rapidly executed of the four harbour views: see especially the summary, cursive treatment interplay between the 'wriggle' and 'brick' strokes in the water enlivens the deep shadows thrown by the buildings. The houses in particular, in their picturesque variety, must have reminded Monet of Honfleur (cf. W 31, 33, 34).

Travel writers and photographers were also attracted by the motif. A stereophotograph, probably of the 1860s, gives a wider, more extensive view, seen straight on (fig. 4). And Henry Havard provided his own drawing of *Les Écluses* as an illustration to his book *Amsterdam and Venice,* published in 1876 (fig. 5). Havard and Monet must often have looked at

this scene together aduring their stay in Zaandam in 1871.

Nothing is known of the early history of this painting. Its first recorded owner, Benoist Lévy, was no relation of the painter Henry Michel-Levý, Monet's companion in Zaandam in June-July 1871. *The Dam on the Achterzaan* later belonged to the English writer W. Somerset Maugham.

4. *Zaandam, the three locks,* c. 1880. Stereoscopic view: Zaandam, Municipal Archives Zaanstad.

5. Maxime Lalanne, *Zaandam: the locks.* From: Henry Havard, *La Hollande à vol d'oiseau,* Paris 1881.

6. *Custom-houses.* Photo by Menko ten Cate, 1986.

111

5 THE ZUIDDIJK WITH THE TOWNHALL AND THE OOSTZIJDERKERK

Oil on canvas, 47.8 x 73 cm
Signed lower left: Claude Monet
W 183
Paris, Musée d'Orsay

The view is taken from the Ganzenwerf looking north across the water with the roof of the town hall visible above the trees next to the tower of the Oostzijderkerk. On the right are the green houses with the red roofs of the Zuiddijk (fig. 7). In the distance, far left, can be seen some of the houses of the Dam.

This is a full summer view of Zaandam, in which Monet has faced the problem of conveying the reflections of sunlight on water, as he had done at La Grenouillère in 1869. This he achieves by the alternation of limpid, transparent areas and shorter, more opaque brick-shaped brushstrokes. This continuation of his observations and reflections can also be seen in the *Houses on the Achterzaan* (cat. no. 9). It seems probable that the two paintings were done at much the same time, probably in August.

As with cat. nos. 1-4, the canvas is a standard French size, 48 x 73 cm. Interestingly, the stretcher has, on its reverse, the stamp of a London colourman, 'Lechertier, Barbe and Co., 7 Glasshouse Street', confirming that Monet brought his materials with him from London.

The painting can probably be identified with that entered in the Durand-Ruel stock book as bought on 30 September 1872, *Village entre les arbres près d'un canal, 300 francs.* It is difficult to identify it with a title used by Monet himself in his *carnet de comptes.*

The first recorded owner after Durand-Ruel was Gustave Goupy, who built up a small but distinguished collection of Impressionist paintings that was sold in Paris on 30 March 1898 (lot 23, *Un canal en Hollande,* sold for 4.400 francs to the art dealer Georges Petit). Soon afterwards, it was acquired by the great collector of 19th-century French painting, Etienne Moreau-Nélaton, and was part of his munificent donation to the Louvre in 1906. It was one of several paintings by Monet shown at the Exposition Universelle in 1900, *Centennale de l'Art Français,* no. 477, *Canal en Hollande: à M. Moreau-Nélaton.* Since entering the Louvre, its title has been simplified to *Zaandam.*

7. *The Zuiddijk*, c. 1870. Photo: Zaandam, Municipal Archives Zaanstad.

6 HOUSES ON THE ACHTERZAAN

Oil on canvas, 44 x 67 cm
Signed and dated lower left: Claude Monet. 72
W 186
New York, Metropolitan Museum of Art, Robert Lehman Collection

Monet's viewpoint in this painting was taken from a landing-stage near the Achterdam, looking north up the Zaan. This part of Zaandam, the Molenbuurt, was one of the richest parts of the town, known in Dutch as 'Fluwelen Westzijde', the 'Velvety Westside'. The houses showed a great variety architectually; and there was considerable freedom in lay-out, so that the constricted regularity and grid-plan of many other parts no longer applied. In addition, these houses facing the street, had, at the bottom of their gardens, facing the river, the typical 'luchthuizen' – literally, airhouses – summer garden houses, as well as small private landing-stages.

A photograph of this stretch of the river Zaan, taken a few years before Monet's painting (fig. 8), provides a clear view of the two 'luchthuizen' visible in the painting. As with the owner main houses, the styles of the 'luchthuizen' varied greatly. The first one visible in the painting was at Westzijde 14.

The inclusion of a pleasure boat, a so-called 'Boeier', on the Zaan is reminiscent of Monet's paintings on the Seine of 1869 (W 136); and prefigures his much greater exploitation of the theme in Argenteuil from 1872 onwards.

This is one of the two paintings of Zaandam that bears a date of 1872 (the other is cat. no. 20). The '72' was added at a later time – it is in a differrent colour – than the signature, probably at the time when Monet sold the picture. As with several of his Zaandam paintings, the early provenance is not known, its first recorded owner being the Paris art dealer Bernheim Jeune in 1910. Nor is there any record of its having been exhibited during Monet's lifetime.

8. *Houses on the Achterzaan*, c. 1870. Photo: Zaandam, Municipal Archives Zaanstad.

7 HOUSES ON THE ACHTERZAAN

Oil on canvas, 44.5 x 65 cm
Signed lower left: Claude Monet
W 187
Private collection

This view, like no. 6, shows the west side of the river Zaan. Monet has now moved further up river to Westzijde 28, but has decided to look South, so that the houses on the Dam are visible in the distance. He almost certainly stood on the small private landing-stage belonging to Antje and Cornelis Van de Stadt-ten Kate, the wooden cantilevered 'luchthuis' being the one belonging to doctor Van der Boom at Westzijde 22.

Several figures are introduced, especially on the river and the landing-stage. The woman in black, holding a pink parasol, is almost certainly Camille Monet. The same woman, in the same dress and with the same parasol, can also be seen in cat. no. 8 (fig. 9).

The 'flavour' of this painting is very French, as if Monet were transposing his summer memories of the Seine at La Grenouillère to the banks of the Zaan. And in that transposing, he emphasized the continuing exploration of 'wriggle and brick' strokes, opaque and trans-

parent, on the water. At the same time, he conveys the structure of the typical Zaandam houses by the river. Fortunately once more, his painted view can be compared with a later picture postcard (fig. 10).

The painting belonged to the single most important collector of Monet's work in the 1870s, the opera singer Jean-Baptiste Faure (1830-1914). It is not known precisely when he acquired it (since its presence cannot be traced with any certainty either in Durand-Ruel's stockbooks or in Monet's *carnet de comptes*). Faure retained the picture until 1901, when he sold it to Durand-Ruel, who shortly afterwards sold it to the great American collector Mrs. H.O. Havemeyer.

9. Detail.

10. *Houses on the Achterzaan*, c. 1900. Postcard: Zaandam, Municipal Archives Zaanstad.

8 GARDEN HOUSE ON THE BANKS OF THE ZAAN

Oil on canvas, 54 x 74 cm
Signed lower right: Claude Monet
W 138
Private collection

Monet's northern progress up the west-side of the river Zaan continues in this painting. From 14 Westzijde (cat. no. 6) and 22 Westzijde (cat. no. 7) we now reach Westzijde 78. The cupola of the luchthuis, as well as its projecting balcony, can be seen in a detail of a later postcard view (fig. 11), which also shows that Monet is looking south-east, across the Zaan. All these houses on the east bank of the river have gone, replaced by factories. In 1871, the luchthuis of 78 Westzijde belonged to Jacob Dam and his wife Aagtje de Lange. Were they friends of the Van de Stadt family? Did Camille give French lessons? We can only speculate.

Camille herself seems to be present again in this painting. Indeed, she is wearing the same dress as she was in the preceding picture: black cloth, white collar and manches, black velvet bow, and a little queue. While her features cannot be distinguished on this scale, she must have been the model in both paintings.

Topographically and in this detail of Camille, this painting has to be placed in Zaandam. Hitherto, it has been thought to be a view on the Seine, its precise location there, however, never made clear. Stylistically it fits far more happily into Monet's Dutch oeuvre of 1871 than it does into his French paintings of either before or after the Franco-Prussian War.

Part of the composition – of the figures in the rowing-boat – recurs in what must be a fragment of another version of this painting (fig. 12). This small fragment, measuring only 18 x 22 cm, but whose figures are on exactly the same scale as those in the present painting, has been included in the *catalogue raisonné* of the work of Berthe Morisot (1961, no. 136, fig. 163, as 'En Barque', 1883). It seems much more probable that it was painted by Monet himself, who then presented the fragment to Berthe Morisot (she also owned the Amsterdam snow scene, cat. no. 36).

11. *Garden house on the banks of the Zaan*, c. 1890. Postcard (detail): Amsterdam, Municipal Archives Amsterdam.

The early history of this painting is unclear. There is no record that Durand-Ruel bought it, and Monet himself did not list it in his *carnet de comptes.*

12. Claude Monet, *En Barque*. From: M.L. Bataille and G. Wildenstein, *Berthe Morisot: Catalogue des peintures, pastels et aquarelles*, Paris 1961.

119

9 HOUSES ON THE ACHTERZAAN

Oil on canvas, 48 x 73.5 cm
Signed lower left: Claude Monet
W 185
Frankfurt am Main, Städelsches Kunstinstitut

After three paintings showing the west bank of the Zaan (cat. nos. 6-8), Monet has here chosen a view of houses on the east bank of the river, the left one of which, an early 17th-century Zaandam House with a typical 18th-century façade, still exists at Oostzijde 221. Monet almost certainly stood on the west bank to make the painting, on the grounds of a gas-factory.

A photograph taken a few years after Monet's painting conveys the distinctive flavour of these houses amid the trees (fig. 14). A recent photograph, adopting Monet's viewpoint, shows the changes that have taken place since 1871 (fig. 15).

This painting is arguably Monet's masterpiece of his Zaandam period. Seldom has his acutely observant eye caught with such absolute conviction the reflections on water; seldom has architecture been rendered so convincingly, despite its potential stage-flatness because of the chosen viewpoint; seldom have sky, foliage, and figures – small accents, but tellingly placed – been united so harmoniously.

13. Léon Gaucherel after Claude Monet, *Houses on the Achterzaan.* From: *Galerie Durand-Ruel, recueil d'estampes,* Paris 1873 (Paris, Archives Durand-Ruel).

120

14. *Houses on the Achterzaan*, c. 1900. Photo: Zaandam, Municipal Archives Zaanstad.

The painting was certainly acquired by Durand-Ruel, since it was published as one of the four etchings after Monet's work in *Galerie Durand-Ruel, recueil d'estampes*, Paris 1873, as no. C1, *Habitations et Canal à Saardam, 48 x 73 cm*, engraved by Gaucherel (fig. 13). It may possibly be identified as one of the twenty-five paintings bought from Monet by Durand-Ruel on 28 February 1873: *2579, Sannedam (Hollande) 400 francs.*

The painting was acquired by the Städelsches Kunstinstitut in 1904, the first Zaandam painting to enter a museum collection.

15. *Oosteinde 221*. Photo by Menko ten Cate, 1986.

121

10 MILLS ALONG THE NOORDERVALDEURSLOOT

Oil on canvas, 46 x 71 cm
Signed lower left: Claude Monet
W 180
Private collection

This small canal runs eastwards at a right angle to the river Zaan some kilometers north of the Dam. The various windmills can be identified: the dye-woodmill 'De Sluiswachter' and the oilmills 'Het Oude Kaar', 'De Quack', 'Het huis te Muiden' and 'De Kaver'.

Monet's view point was almost certainly from the lock on the Noordervaldeursloot. The motif was often photographed and also used in postcards of Zaandam. One of these postcards (fig. 16) is taken closer in than Monet's painting, but it shows once again how faithful Monet was to his chosen motif.

It seems probable that the rapid drawing of two windmills that Monet made on one of his sketchbook pages shows the two foreground mills in the painting, but without being a preliminary study for them (Musée Marmottan, folio 30; fig. 17).

The early history of the painting is uncertain. But it was certainly in an American collection by the 1890s, that of the New Jersey industrialist Catholina Lambert (1834-1923).

122

16. *Mills along the Noordervaldeursloot,* c. 1890. Postcard: Zaandam, Municipal Archives Amsterdam.

17. Claude Monet, *Mills.* Paris, Musée Marmottan.

11 THE ZAAN NEAR ZAANDAM

Oil on canvas, 42 x 73 cm
Signed lower left: Claude Monet
W 172
Private collection

The view shows part of the river Zaan between Zaandam and Koog, looking north, as the river bends in a slow right curve towards the Hemmes. The windmills can be identified: on the left, the Kogeroever with the oil-mill 'The Giant'; on the right bank, the 'Young Lady' and the 'Nobleman' and further away 'The Wheel of Fortune', 'The Green Farmer' and the mills on the Hemmes. According to Frans Mars in 'Claude Monet', *Zaandam 150 jaar stad*, Zaandam 1962, pp. 331-33, Monet has painted the mills as if the wind were in the west, and the boats as if the wind were in the east.

Does this suggest a 'composed' picture? Some confirmation of this may be found in the sketchbook drawing of a fishing-boat (Musée Marmottan, folio 31, see fig. 19), which must have formed the basis for the fishing-boat in the painting. Did Monet add the boat later, thus producing the inconsistencies in wind direction? With the fishing-boat placed so deliberately, and with an open foreground, the composition has an old-fashioned look about it, one that Jongkind or Daubigny might have painted. Of course, the range of reds that Monet plays with across the surface of the painting, the bold

strokes that 'build' up the water, and the similar, but looser 'brick' strokes in the sky all proclaim his technical audacity.

The painting was acquired by Durand-Ruel on 11 May 1872: stock no. 1693 *Moulins à Hollande* for 300 francs. It was sold to Daubigny in January 1873 for 800 francs. Daubigny, with his artist-son Karl (1846-1886) was in Holland in September 1871. With observations and sketches, he then returned to Paris where he produced a large painting for the Salon of 1872 (fig. 27, under cat. no. 22). Monet's painting was one of the four etched in *Galerie Durand-Ruel, receuil d'estampes* (1873), as no. V *Moulins en Hollande* (fig. 18).

After Daubigny's death in 1878, the painting was included in his studio sale of May 1878, where it was acquired by the art critic and collector Théodore Duret for the small sum of 80 francs. Monet asked Duret for its loan to his first major one-man show at the Galleries of Durand-Ruel in May 1883 (where it was wrongly called 'Un canal à Zaandam'); and again for his large show that he shared with Rodin at the Galerie Petit in 1889. This for him, therefore, was an important painting.

124

18. Léon Gaucherel after Claude Monet, *The Zaan near Zaandam*. From: *Galerie Durand Ruel, recueil d'estampes*, Paris 1873. (Paris, Archives Durand-Ruel).

19. Claude Monet, *Fishing-boat*. Paris, Musée Marmottan.

12 THE ZAAN NEAR ZAANDAM

Oil on canvas, 35.2 x 71 cm
Signed lower right: Claude Monet
W 173
The Glynn Vivian Art Gallery, Swansea Museum Service

This view on the Żaan is comparable to that in the preceding painting. Monet, however, is not quite so far north, thus giving a larger view of the distant bank. There are other differences – if not discrepancies – between the two paintings, most particularly in the number and disposition of the windmills. For example, the pair of windmills on the right bank, so prominent in cat. no. 11, is here reduced to one. But a close examination of the surface of the Swansea painting indicates that this area has been repainted (see especially the houses nearby the windmill); a second windmill may initially have been there. Paradoxically, on the opposite (west) bank, Monet initially had a second windmill to the right of the existing one, which he proceeded to paint out during the course of working. In the distance, there appear to be fewer mills than in cat. no. 11; but the disposition of the fishing-boats, the greater distance, and the grey overcast weather may account for this.

If cat. no. 11 was a 'composed' picture, the Swansea painting is more audaciously 'modern', with its cutting of the boat and the mooring post at the lower left, and the greater sense of immediacy that is induced by the movement of the boat on the river. This painting could be called his, freely and informally observed, rapidly and confidently painted. The other painting could be called a selling or an exhibition picture: yet, ironically, it was an artist, Daubigny, who bought it.

The early history of the painting is unknown. It might be identified with the *Bateaux de pêche, Zaandam* that Monet listed in his *carnet de comptes* as sold to Durand-Ruel for 300 francs in 1872, without indicating a month. No comparable entry occurs in Durand-Ruel's stockbook.

126

13 MILLS IN THE WESTZIJDERVELD

Oil on canvas, 47 x 73 cm
Signed lower left: Claude Monet
W 181
United States, William Kelly Simpson

These windmills stood in the polderland to the West of Zaandam, in the Westzijderveld. They are part of a veritable proliferation of canals and windmills in this area, as can be seen from a sketchbook drawing by Monet (Musée Marmottan, folio 33; fig. 20). Hence, it is virtually impossible to say which canal is depicted, in which direction Monet looked, and whether, as Wildenstein suggests, the season is autumn.

What is certain, however, is that this is one of Monet's most direct and confident paintings of Zaandam. Mass and silhouette, volume and fragility are conveyed with the utmost economy. A light wind ripples the water – and Monet finds a simple pictorial convention to render the effect that he does not use elsewhere in his Zaandam paintings. The large, almost 'abstract' brick-shaped strokes that he uses in the sky prefigure some of Mondrian's early landscapes. It is probably late afternoon. All these elements create a contrast with this painting's pair, cat. no. 14.

The early history of this picture is unclear. Its first certain owner was the German painter Max Liebermann (1847-1935). Coincidentally, he too was in Holland in September 1871: he signed the *livre d'or* of the Trippenhuis in Amsterdam on 11 and 12 September.

14 MILLS IN THE WESTZIJDERVELD

Oil on canvas, 48 x 73 cm
Signed lower right: Claude Monet
W 182
Private collection

As in the preceding painting, these windmills stood to the west of Zaandam, in the Westzijderveld. Monet almost certainly looked west, towards a tempered sunset, whose sky and silhouetted windmills seem to presage some of Mondrian's early landscapes.

By comparison with cat. no. 13, it demonstrates the ease of Monet's adaptability to a different time of day and different weather effects. Here, all is still; no boats, just one figure crossing the fragile, Japanese-like footbridge, reflections rendered as flat wash and gentle hatching, a colour scheme that is subdued, cool, green-dominant.

The picture's first recorded owner was Charles Deudon, who assembled a small but very distinguished collection of Monet's work, as well as that of Manet and Renoir. It was Deudon who made the introduction to Baron d'Estournelles de Constant, enabling Monet to visit Holland in April 1886 and paint the bulb fields (see cat. nos. 38-42).

20. Claude Monet, *Mills in the Westzijderveld*. Paris, Musée Marmottan.

15 THE BLUE HOUSE ON THE HOGENDIJK

Oil on canvas, 46 x 61 cm
Signed bottom left: Claude Monet
W 184
Present whereabouts unknown

The view is looking west along the Hogendijk, no. 78 is the 'Blue House', on the left is the Voorzaan. While the house is still recognisable, the surroundings have been considerably transformed (figs. 21 and 22). Travel writers frequently alluded to the variety of colours to be found in Zaandam houses: red and green (cf. cat. no. 5), blue and orange. Part of the startling nature of this painting is therefore attributable to the things seen. Monet has accepted the uninterupted one colour of the house, virtually without shadow. Is this just his natural, honest vision, or is it partly the influence of Japanese woodblock prints?

Even the shadow of the fence could be read as darkening of the gravel. The foliage, especially that of the light coloured tree in the garden, suggests June: not yet full-blown summer. One of the two female figures must surely be Camille with her son Jean, then almost four years old. It is their sole appearance together in a Zaandam

painting: Monet had used them together in streetscenes before 1870 (e.g. W 152); and once settled in Argenteuil, he frequently introduced them into his paintings (see W 274, 280, 282).

The painting was bought by Durand-Ruel in April 1872: stock number 1254, *La Maison bleue, 300 fr.* Monet also recorded the transaction in his *carnet de comptes,* using the same title. It soon entered the collection of Ernest Hoschedé (1837-1891), but it was included in his sale of 13 January 1874 (lot 45, 405 francs, bought by Baudry). Monet, working in Le Havre in January 1874, wrote to Pissarro about the Hoschedé sale: 'I very much regret not being there myself in order to buy back my *Blue House* to which I am very attached.' It was the only Dutch painting by Monet to be included in the Impressionist exhibitions, figuring in the fourth show of 1879 as *Habitation Bourgeoise, à Zaandum* (sic), *Hollande. Appartient à Mr. Baudry.* Subsequently, Monet included it, *hors*

130

21. *Side-view of the Blue house.* Photo by Menko ten Cate, 1986.

catalogue, in his one-man show at Durand-Ruel in 1883.

It is one of only two of Monet's Dutch pictures to have belonged to a Dutch collector, M.P. Voûte Jr. (1882-1955) of Baarn. This merchant, who was vice-president of the Vereniging Rembrandt, lent it to the large exhibition of French art held at the Stedelijk Museum, Amsterdam in July-September 1938 (cat. no. 173). Voûte also owned one of the bulb fields (see cat. no. 40).

22. *Frontal of the Blue house.* Photo by Menko ten Cate, 1986.

131

16 THE VOORZAAN AND THE WESTERHEM

Oil on canvas, 18.3 x 38.5 cm
Stamped signature lower right: Claude Monet
W 176
Private collection

This view together with cat. nos. 17 and 18, was painted from a landing-stage on the west side of the harbour, near the Dam, looking south. Across the water lies the 'Westerhem', the island in the Voorzaan. Compare the photograph (fig. 23).

These three paintings show variations in Monet's response to the given motif. A planar disposition of sea, land and sky is then given different accents in the disposition of fishing boats. The present one is his only small *pochade* from Zaandam, surprising in its range of colour, being far from monochromatic. It never left Monet's studio.

23. *The Voorzaan and the Westerhem*, c. 1880. Photo (detail): Zaandam, Municipal Archives Zaanstad.

132

17 THE VOORZAAN AND THE WESTERHEM

Oil on canvas, 39 x 71.2 cm
Stamped signature lower right: Claude Monet
W 175
Private collection

Here, Monet reverts to one of his usual size canvases; adjusts the colour range to the prevailing weather conditions; and shifts the position of the two boats: an almost Whistlerian study in tone, economy of statement, and placement of elements. The painting is probably based on the small *pochade*. Like cat. no. 16, it never left Monet's studio.

18. THE VOORZAAN AND THE WESTERHEM

Oil on canvas, 34 x 73.3 cm
Signed lower right: Claude Monet
W 174
Private collection

In this third version of the same motif Monet has added two more fishing boats, and further complicated the simplicity of the composition by adding the moored boats with figures in the foreground, dramatically cut by the edges of the canvas. A similar device of inducing immediacy and informality was used in the Swansea painting (cat. no. 12); before Zaandam, Monet used the device in his paintings of La Grenouillère of 1869 (W 134-136).

The painting was made with great speed, almost certainly completed in one session on the spot. Its early history is uncertain. But when sold by an anonymous owner in Paris on 28 November 1924, it was called *Bords de la Meuse, en Hollande, temps gris*. So far, however, no evidence exists that Monet ever painted this river.

At the 1886 Impressionist exhibition in New York, the Philadelphia collector Alexander Cassatt lent two marine paintings by Monet that went under the titles of *Banks of the Meuse, Holland* and *Boats on the Meuse, Holland* (cat. nos. 302-3). It has been suggested by Wildenstein that the present painting was one of these works. Cassatt's collection was purchased with the advice and help of his sister, the painter Mary Cassatt (1844-1926), who may also have been instrumental in his acquiring the *Marine View in Holland* by Edouard Manet (p. 23, fig.

9). This work, again, was called *Boats on the Meuse, Holland* in the exhibition catalogue of 1886 (cat. no. 298).

134

19 FOOTBRIDGE

Oil on canvas, 46 x 38 cm
Inscribed lower right: à l'ami H.H. C. Monet 71 Zaandam
Not in Wildenstein
Macon, Musée Municipal des Ursulines

24. *Small street in Zaandam*, c. 1880. Photo: Zaandam, Municipal Archives Zaanstad.

The motif is difficult to identify, but probably was to be found off the Zuiddijk (where the Van de Stadt family lived), part of which can be seen in cat. no. 5. The photograph (fig. 24) gives a comparable picturesque part of Zaandam.

This small painting is unique in several ways. It commemorates the friendship between Monet and the art critic, art historian, and travel writer Henry Havard (1838-1921) that appears to have been confined to their stay in Zaandam in 1871. There is no subsequent evidence of their maintaining the contact; and in his reviews of Monet's paintings at the 4th Impressionist exhibition of 1879 and at the 7th exhibition of 1882, both in the newspaper *Le Siècle*, Havard confessed himself unable to comprehend Monet's style and vision. Havard himself was a pronounced Dutchophile, writing several books on Holland and Amsterdam, as well as on Vermeer, on *l'Art et les artistes hollandais* (1879- 81), and on *La Faience de Delft* (1878).

This small painting, dedicated to Havard, captures a corner of a typical, picturesque Dutch scene, even including the woman in the doorway; and in so doing Monet has surely selected the motif and adjusted his handling of it to suit Havard's taste. Apart from the *Portrait*

of Guurtje van de Stadt (see cat. no. 25), it is the only painting of Monet disposed of during his stay in Zaandam. Havard left Zaandam before the end of July and the painting must therefore date from the first weeks of Monet's stay.

The painting is also unique in its size (46 x 38 cm); and also as a small upright that contrasts with the horizontal formats of all the other Zaandam landscapes.

Despite his doubts about the later Monet Havard kept the painting and bequeathed it to the Musée Municipal des Ursulines in 1921. In an inventory of his collection, it appeared as *Passerelle près d'un cottage, tableau par Monet, avec dédice*. Havard's favourite painting of Holland was a small view of Haarlem by Léopold Flameng (1831-1911) (illustrated in Havard's article on Flameng, *La Revue de l'Art Ancien et Moderne*, July-Dec. 1903, p. 459). In addition, the inventory listed a *Paysage Hollandais*, also dedicated to Havard, by Emile Vernier (1829-87); and *Vue d'Utrecht*, a charcoal drawing by Maxime Lalanne (1827-1886).

Oil on canvas, 48 x 73.5 cm
Signed and dated lower right: 72 Claude Monet
W 177
Present whereabouts unknown

The dye-woodmill known as 'Het Oosterkatte-gat' used to stand on the land outside the Zuid-dijk, near to the present Prins Hendrikstraat. Monet has painted it looking from north to south. The open water to the right is that of the Voorzaan and the IJ.

Monet's evocation of evening, by use of sil-houette, long shadow, still, unruffled water is comparable to the same effects that he achieved in cat. no. 14. In the present picture, however, he gives the *effet de coucher du Soleil* an addi-tional point by including the flock of birds. The thin and the fragile - ship's mast and flag, reeds and grasses, and poles - contrast with the larger masses of windmill, ship sails and rowing boats. Its very informality, its supreme simplicity, its apparent spontaneity do not disguise Monet's guile in pictorial orchestration. It seems most probable that he painted it from a boat. For a view of the same motif, see cat. no. 21.

This was the second Zaandam painting ac-quired by the operatic baritone Jean-Baptiste Faure (cf. cat. no. 7). He lent it to Monet's im-portant one-man show at Durand-Ruel in 1883,

25. Claude Monet, *Holland*. From: T. Duret, *Histoire des peintres impressionnistes*, Paris 1919.

when a drawing after it on Gillot paper was made; and again to the Monet-Rodin show in 1889 (fig. 25).

21 THE MILL
'HET OOSTERKATTEGAT'

Oil on canvas, 42 x 73.3 cm
Signed lower right: Claude Monet
W 178
Oxford, The Visitors of the Ashmolean Museum

This view shows the same windmill and a larger stretch of the Voorzaan and the IJ as in the preceding painting. Monet, however, has moved his vantage-point closer to the mill itself, and created a different relationship between the mill and the boats. The sail of the boat at sea is crucial to the composition; yet close examination of the painted surface to the right of the windmill suggests that another large sail (probably red) was once part of Monet's design, which he eliminated during the course of working.

Compositional adjustments were made by Monet, even though this supremely fresh and immediate painting suggests the opposite. In its contrast to cat. no. 20 it recalls the treatment of cat. no. 13, as against its pair, cat. no. 14.

26. *The mill 'Het Oosterkattegat'*, c. 1880. Photo: Zaandam, Municipal Archives Zaanstad.

22 THE MILL
'HET OOSTERKATTEGAT'

Oil on canvas, 48.5 x 73.5 cm
Signed lower left: Claude Monet
W 171
The Earl of Jersey

This is a third view of the mill 'Het Oosterkatte-gat' (cf. cat. nos. 20-21). Monet has taken the view looking north – in the distance can be seen the tower of the Oostzijderkerk (cf. cat. no. 5). The boats belonged to the fishing fleet of Zaandam: here was their home harbour.

A photograph of the mill (fig. 26), taken at approximately the same time, shows once more how closely Monet stuck to the motif before him.

Monet has composed his picture, using an open foreground, a focus of interest around the mill, and a distant prospect of the town. It is a compositional formula close to that often used by Jongkind, for instance in an etching of 1867 (fig. 28). If there were a painting that Monet might have thought of as a possible submission to the Salon of 1872 then this could have been it; compare Daubigny's Salon painting of 1872 (fig. 27). As well as being carefully composed, the painting is less hurriedly executed than the majority of Monet's Zaandam oeuvre. The colour scheme is muted also.

The painting was bought by Durand-Ruel in 1872 or 1873; there is no easily identifiable title that corresponds to the painting in the stockbooks. But it was one of the three Dutch subjects by Monet chosen for illustration in the 1873 publication *Galerie Durand-Ruel, recueil d'estampes*, where it was no. CXLVII *Moulins et Marais en Hollande 54 x 75 cm*, etched by Flameng (fig. 29). It is particularly interesting that the etching was done by Léopold Flameng (1831-1911), who was a friend of Henry Havard, and much admired by him (cf. cat. no. 19).

This was the first of Monet's Dutch paintings to be exhibited in Holland – in October 1893 at the Haagsche Kunstkring in The Hague.

27. Charles Daubigny, *Mills near Dordrecht*, 1872. Detroit, Detroit Institute of Arts.

28. Johan Bartold Jongkind, *Mills in Holland*, 1867. The Hague, Municipal Museum.

29. Léopold Flameng after Claude Monet, *The Mill 'Het Oosterkattegat'*. From: *Galerie Durand-Ruel, recueil d'estampes*, Paris 1873 (Paris, Durand-Ruel Archives).

23 THE WEERPAD NEAR ZAANDAM

Oil on canvas, 40 x 72 cm
Signed lower right: Claude Monet
W 170
Baltimore, Walters Art Gallery

The Weerpad, that runs in the direction of Oostzaan, lies to the south-east of Zaandam, and Monet has viewed it looking east. A photo of about 1900 shows a comparable view of the area (fig. 30). In the distance its church tower can be seen behind the large flourmill 'Het Oosterzanerwapen'. The two mills in the foreground of the meadow on the right have not been identified. The three windmills however, are known. They bear the poetical names of 'Waking', 'Sleeping' and 'Dreaming'.

Of all Monet's views of Zaandam, this is closest in its grey-green tonalities to Corot and the Barbizon artists, and in that sense it is nearest to some of the Hague school painters. But it also owes something to Monet's London paintings and its restrained tonalities suggest that it might be a relatively early painting of Zaandam.

Monet enlivens the scene by adding the figure of a girl wearing local costume and carrying buckets suspended from a yoke as she crosses the footbridge; while beyond her is a figure in a rowing boat.

As with several of Monet's Zaandam paintings, the early history of the Baltimore picture is uncertain. Although it carries on its reverse a paper label marked 'Durand-Ruel, Moulins en Hollande 1874', there is evidently no trace of the painting in the Durand-Ruel archives. All that is certain is that the great American collector Henry Walters (1848-1931) acquired it after 1909.

30. *The Weerpad*, c. 1900. Photo: Zaandam, Municipal Archives Zaanstad.

140

24 THE VOORZAAN AND THE IJ

Oil on canvas, 34 x 74 cm
Signed lower right: Claude Monet
W 179
Stockholm, Nationalmuseum

The view shows the joining of the Voorzaan and the IJ to the South of Zaandam. This is the furthest south of Zaandam that Monet actually painted.

The painting looks spontaneous and fresh. Yet the boat in full sail is very close to that in the Oxford painting (cat. no. 21). Coincidence? Or Monet using an existing 'pose'? Yet who more than Monet knew boats of all descriptions, painted them in all seasons, in all weathers, in storm, in harbour. Manet called him 'The Raphaël of the water': the *mot* was quoted in a newsaper review of 1879 (see Charles S. Moffett (ed.), *The New Painting,* Oxford 1986, p. 252).

The Stockholm painting bears out Monet's claim. Biographically, it would be the last view of Zaandam that Monet had when he took the boat to Amsterdam on 8 October 1871.

This painting returned to Amsterdam in 1912, when it was included in the large *Exposition internationale des beaux-arts* at the Stedelijk Museum (cat. no. 417). Its early history is unclear, but it first surfaced in the Paris sale room in 1900. It entered the Nationalmuseum in Stockholm in 1926.

25 PORTRAIT OF GUURTJE VAN DE STADT

Oil on canvas, 73 x 40 cm
Signed and dated lower left: C. Monet 1871
W 192
Otterlo, Rijksmuseum Kröller -Müller

It is not known how Monet became acquainted with the Van de Stadt family. But it may well have been through Camille Monet, who gave lessons in French conversation. Since the early nineteenth century, their business had been in timber, which helped place them among the more prosperous families in Zaandam. In 1871, they lived on the Zuiddijk. This dike can be seen in cat. no. 5.

In April 1871, Jan van de Stadt died at the age of forty-five. He left eight children, four boys and four girls. Guurtje was born on 20 October 1854. She was almost seventeen years old when Monet painted her portrait. She is still dressed in mourning for her father: a wide sleeved dress, possibly slightly too big for her, 'gitten' earrings and a black bow in her hair. A photograph, taken approximately at the same time, shows her in a different way (fig. 31). She married in 1878 E.G. Duyvis, oil-miller from Koog on the Zaan, and died in 1936.

Monet's portrait, uncharacteristically for him an 'arrangement' of black and grey, was conditioned by the family's continuing mourning. Monet rarely undertook commissioned portraits *(Mme Gaudibert,* W 121, of 1868 is a significant exception); and his sole Dutch portrait did not allow him to express himself forcefully.

Interestingly, the Dutch artist A.H. Koning (1860-1945) wrote of the van de Stadt family and Monet in an unpublished letter to Vincent van Gogh of 15 February 1889 (Amsterdam, Rijksmuseum Vincent van Gogh): 'Concerning the latter master (Claude Monet) - Some days ago I was with my Roessingh relatives in Haarlem and as usual the conversation was of art and artists when my cousin Cato van der Stadt suddenly remarked "Yes, we also know a French painter and his wife who used to come and paint in Zaandam. They are great friends of ours and of our relations in Zaandam", and by such a stroke of luck I found there in Haarlem, in my cousin's album, the portraits of Claude Monet and his wife'. These portraits stayed in the family, and are here published for the first time (p. 45, figs. 30, 31).

31. *Guurtje van de Stadt,* 1870-1871. Photo: Private Collection.

MAP OF AMSTERDAM
Reconstructed after a map of 1873.
The numbers refer to the catalogue entries.

AMSTERDAM

Very little is known of Monet's presence in Amsterdam. The only documentation refers to events in 1871: his signing of the visitor's book in the Trippenhuis on 22 June, photographs of him and Camille taken by the well-known Amsterdam photographer, A. Greiner; and his brief passage through the city after leaving Zaandam on 8 October.

The major testimony to his presence are the twelve surviving paintings. These raise several problems. Although they are all signed, not one is dated. None was bought by Durand-Ruel in the 1870s; and none was entered into Monet's *carnet de comptes* with a clear and unequivocal Amsterdam title. Nor did Monet include any of them in exhibitions – either Impressionist group or one-man shows – of the 1870s and 1880s.

Yet, by the 1880s, the vast majority of them had entered important private collections of Monet's work. Two belonged to the Comte and Comtesse de Rasty (cat. nos. 27 and 37) among some five of his paintings. The extensive view of the IJ (cat. no. 26) was owned by Charles Leroux, a prominent collector in Nantes, who already had at least ten works by Monet. The banker Ernest May, owner of one Zaandam picture (cat. no. 2), bought the largest of the Amsterdam canvases (cat. no. 31). Eugène Murer, pastrycook, painter and writer, acquired a small variation of May's picture, probably as early as 1877 (cat. no. 32). Dr. de Bellio, the Rumanian-born homeopath, and one of Monet's staunchest patrons in the 1870s, bought one of the two contrasting views of the *Groenburgwal with the Zuiderkerk* (cat. no. 33); while the other was acquired by the family of Mary Cassatt in Philadelphia (cat. no. 34). Another Impressionist painter, Berthe Morisot, owned one of the two snowscenes (cat. no. 36), although it is not known how and when she acquired it. The earliest recorded acquisition was of the *Montelbaanstoren on the Rapenburgwal* (cat. no. 29) bought in Paris in 1875 by Louisine Waldron Elder (later Mrs. H.O. Havemeyer) on the advice of Mary Cassatt. All this means that the early history of only three of the Amsterdam pictures (cat. nos. 28, 30, 35) is unknown. But it does seem probable that all

twelve had left Monet's studio by the 1880s.

Topographically, Monet's choices of motif often form clusters round specific areas of the city, as the map shows. One such cluster shows views of the IJ and of houses overlooking the port (cat. nos. 26, 27, 31, 32); another takes in three views on the Binnen-Amstel canal (cat. nos. 30, 33, 34); yet another depicts variations on the Montelbaanstoren (cat. nos. 28, 29). Many were overtly tourist views, frequently reproduced in guidebooks, etched, lithographed and photographed. One of the most popular was the Roozeboom Mill, some distance from the other motifs (cat. no. 35). Monet's two snowscapes of Amsterdam are also separate confrontations, one of the Gelderse Kade (cat. no. 36), the other of the Westerdok (cat. no. 37).

Stylistically, the Amsterdam landscapes bear little relationship to those of Zaandam. Sizes and formats differ. The long horizontals favoured by Monet in Zaandam are gone. The Amsterdam canvases tend to be squarer and larger. One in particular, the largest, is equivalent to the pairs of landscapes Monet produced in Argenteuil and Le Havre in 1873-74 (see the entry for cat. no. 31).

What has changed above all is the handling and the colour. Brushstrokes are more abrupt and dynamic and applied in shorthand, that places the Amsterdam paintings among the true manifestations of Impressionist technique. Such was the rapidity of Monet's touch – or series of *taches,* one might say – that the prepared ground of the canvas, whether grey (as in cat. nos. 27 and 28) or tan (as in cat. nos. 33 and 34) was often allowed to show through, acting at times as part of the colour scheme. This audaciously abbreviated and suggestive treatment implies a date of 1873 or 1874 for the Amsterdam paintings.

They probably represent more than one visit. In the two views of the Groenburgwal and the Zuiderkerk (cat. nos. 33 and 34) it would appear to be autumn, whereas the trees in the two views of the Kamperhoofd (cat. nos. 31 and 32) suggest winter. And then there are the two snowscenes (cat. nos. 36 and 37). Monet's stays in Amsterdam were probably brief, a week or ten days at most. Not a scrap of contemporary evidence has come to light: no police records, now that the political fears surrounding the Commune had passed, no visits to the Trippenhuis or to the photographer's studio. And topographical changes, such as the demolition of the 'Roozeboom' windmill in October 1876 (see cat. no. 35), do not help in dating the paintings.

No other group of Monet's paintings from the 1870s – or, indeed, from any part of his career – so completely lacks documentation.

Because of their fairly rapid disappearance into private collections and because Monet never chose to exhibit any of them, the Amsterdam group of painting received virtually no mention in the early literature on the artist. It was not until 1925 that one was reproduced in a periodical published in Paris. They were first brought together in Daniel Wildenstein's *catalogue raisonné* of 1974. Only since then has it been possible to see them as a whole. But, even now, each stubbornly retains its secret.

32. Jacob Maris, *The Buiten IJ*, 1873. Laren, Singer Museum.

146

26 THE IJ

Oil on canvas, 50.5 x 75.5 cm
Signed lower left: Claude Monet
W 299
Private collection

This view of the IJ is probably taken from the Stadsherberg, looking east, with the tower of Ransdorp in the far distance. Such an extensive view of the harbour with three-mast ships contrasting with fishing boats and smaller craft was not new in Monet's oeuvre. Compare his large Salon painting of 1865, *L'Embouchère de la Seine à Honfleur* (W 51), as well as *Impression, Soleil levant* of 1873 (W 263) and especially two contrasting views of the former *avant-port du Havre* (W 296 and 297), observed in rain and sunshine and painted in 1874.

The style of the Amsterdam painting suggests, in its economy of means, its deft, rapid brush strokes, and general thinness of paint, a relative closeness to the two Le Havre paintings of January 1874.

For a view virtually contemporary with it, compare the 1873 dated view of the Buiten-IJ by Jacob Maris, now in the Singer Museum, Laren (fig. 32).

The first recorded owner of the painting was a Nantes collector, Charles Leroux. He as-sembled some ten paintings by Monet in the 1880s, eight of which were included in his sale on 27 February 1888.

27. THE IJ

Oil on canvas, 60 x 81 cm
Signed lower right: Claude Monet
W 298
Private collection

This view of the port of Amsterdam is, like cat. no. 26, not without its parallels and prototypes in Monet's work. Such relatively close views of boats in harbour were made in the 1860s at Le Havre (W 76) and Fécamp (W 116); and they recur in paintings of Rouen in 1872-73 (W 210, and especially W 267). But what distinguishes the Amsterdam painting from the rest is Monet's supremely economical statement. Monet has painted on a grey prepared ground, and allowed that ground to show in many parts of the painting. Over it, he has rapidly indicated boats, water, and sky, in a range of colours different from Zaandam: red, yellow, blue, orange and green combine to create volume, shape, texture, air, light, reflection in a series of almost abstracts marks. In all these respects, it forms a pair with *The Montelbaanstoren* (cat. no. 28).

The first recorded owner of the painting were the Comte and Comtesse Jean de Rasty.

Among their four other paintings by Monet was a snowscene of Amsterdam (cat. no. 37).

33. *The Montelbaanstoren*, c. 1890. Photo: Amsterdam, Municipal Archives.

148

28 THE MONTELBAANSTOREN ON THE OUDE SCHANS

Oil on canvas, 60 x 81 cm
Signed lower right: Claude Monet
W 307
Private collection

Monet probably painted this view from a moored boat in front of the Keizersbrug, looking north. A photograph of the same motif shows how Monet has accurately observed the recession from the Oude Schans to the Binnenkant and the Kalkmarkt (fig. 33). In the right background lies the Kikkerbilsluis with the Oosterdok beyond – where large ships similar to those in the preceding painting (cat. no. 27) can be seen.

Indeed, the connection between the two paintings is very close. They are both painted on identical size canvases, with the same greyprepared ground, on which a series of high speed strokes, using the same red, orange, yellow and blue (but not green) and allowing more of the grey ground to show – for instance, in the tower and in the façade of the houses. All this suggests that Monet could have produced both paintings on the same day.

The early history of the painting is unknown, but it was with Durand-Ruel by 1891. Its first recorded inclusion in an exhibition was in that of the Vereeniging voor de Kunst in Utrecht in early 1901.

149

29 THE MONTELBAANSTOREN AND THE RAPENBURGWAL

Oil on canvas, 53.5 x 63.5 cm
Signed lower right: Claude Monet
W 306
Shelburne, Vermont, Shelburne Museum

Although the Montelbaanstoren, seen in the preceding painting (cat. no. 28), reappears here, it has been viewed from a different canal. Monet is facing the Peperbrug across the Rapenburgwal, beneath which can be seen another bridge, the Torenbrug, across the Waalseiland gracht, be it without its elevated part. The view is almost certainly painted from a boat. The motif, with variations caused by a different viewpoint, can be seen in a contemporary photograph (fig. 34).

As well as changing his viewpoint, Monet has also changed his palette and his brushstrokes to suit the change in the weather. Overcast sky and rain - hence figures with umbrellas - have caused him to abandon the primary colours that alone built up the scene so summarily

in the preceding pair of paintings (cat. nos. 27, 28). Here, he works over a whitish prepared canvas, and actually began with a chalk underdrawing that is especially visible in and around the drawbridge, where pentimenti can be detected. Nevertheless, the painting was executed very rapidly: note the treatment of the façade of the houses at the left, and more so the way in which some figures crossing the bridge are actually in front of the rails (this 'impossible' placement of the figures can also be seen in the New York version of *La Grenouillère* of 1869, W 134, illustrated on page 51 of this catalogue). Indeed, the colour of the water, and the combination of 'wriggle and brick' strokes are reminiscent of the La Grenouillère series, as well as of certain paintings of Zaandam. Yet on

150

34. *The Montelbaanstoren and the Rapenburgwal*, c. 1870-1880. Photo: Amsterdam, Municipal Archives.

balance a date of 1873 seems preferable to one of October 1871.

This was Monet's first painting to be acquired by an American collector. Louisine Elder, later Mrs. H.O. Havemeyer, bought it in Paris in 1875 for 300 francs, on the advice of Mary Cassatt. (See Frances Weitzenhoffer, 'The earliest American collectors of Monet', in: *Aspects of Monet*, eds. John Rewald and Frances Weitzenhoffer, New York 1984, p. 78.)

30 THE BINNEN-AMSTEL AND THE MUNTTOREN

Oil on canvas, 55 x 74 cm
Signed lower left: Claude Monet
W 305
Private collection

Monet painted this view on the Binnen-Amstel, probably from one of the barges, looking west towards the Halvemaans bridge, with the Munttoren to the left. Postcard views establish ·the main elements of Monet's composition (fig. 35, 36).

Known only from an indifferent black-and-white photograph, this painting seems,to be close in *facture* to the preceding one (cat. no. 29). Almost on the same spot that Monet painted this view, be it closer to the quay, he turned 90 degrees and produced the two views of the Groenburgwal with the Zuiderkerk (cat. nos. 33 and 34).

The early history of the present painting is unknown. It first appeared at the Van Houten sale in Paris on 12 June 1953 (lot 11).

35. *The Binnen-Amstel and the Munttoren*, c. 1900. Photo: Amsterdam, Municipal Archives.

36. *The Binnen-Amstel and the Munttoren*, c. 1870-1880. Photo: Amsterdam, Municipal Archives.

Oil on canvas, 61 x 101.5 cm
Signed lower left: Claude Monet
W 303
Private collection

Monet stood at the beginning of the Ooster-doksdijk and looked west. Behind the trees is the Schreierstoren. Today, this is part of the Prins Hendrikkade. A stereophotograph shows the same motif, with a slight variation in the viewing angle (fig. 37).

Monet has used the same abrupt, sugges-tive handling that characterised the preceding Amsterdam paintings. What makes the present picture unique among his Amsterdam oeuvre is its particular format and large size – 60 x 100 cm. This is a canvas size that Monet began using in 1873, in two spring landscapes of Argenteuil (W 271-272), continued to use for two snow-scenes of Argentueil (W 388-389) and two con-trasting views of the harbour at Le Havre of January 1874 (W 295 and W 296). The Amster-dam painting, therefore, fits into this larger pat-tern.

Its first recorded owner was the banker Er-nest May (1845-1923), who had at least nine paintings by Monet, among them the view of Zaandam harbour (see cat. no. 2).

37. *The Kamperhoofd*, c. 1870-1880. Stereoscopic view: Amsterdam, Municipal Archives.

32 THE KAMPERHOOFD AND THE OUDE WAAL

Oil on canvas, 50 x 68 cm
Signed lower right: Claude Monet
W 304
Private collection

Monet probably sat on a ship near the Oosterdoksdijk and looked from north to south. This part is now called Prins Hendrikkade. The motif was round the corner from the view in the preceding painting: the same trees are visible in both paintings.

Known only from a black-and-white photograph, this small painting apparently shares comparable features in the handling of water and buildings with cat. nos. 29 and 30.

Monet classed it as a *pochade*, a rapidly executed sketch done on the spot. It was acquired by the pastrycook, painter and writer Eugène Murer (1846-1906), probably in 1877, one of a vast number of paintings he eventually owned by Monet, Renoir, Pissarro, Sisley, Cézanne and Guillaumin.

155

33 THE GROENBURGWAL AND THE ZUIDERKERK

Oil on canvas, 55.6 x 65 cm
Signed lower right: Claude Monet
W 308
Collection d'Arschot

This was an extremely popular tourist view, frequently illustrated in a variety of media (fig. 38). Monet probably stood on the same barge on the Binnen-Amstel that he used to paint the Binnen-Amstel and the Munttoren (cat. no. 30); he has simply turned 90 degrees to look up the Groenburgwal. On the left, is a ferryman's house that served the 's-Gravelandse ferry.

This painting must have been conceived quite deliberately as a pair to cat. no. 34. Each is painted on an identical size canvas, bearing the Paris artist colourman's stamp of Alexis Ottoz on its reverse. (This is still visible on the present canvas, which has not been relined.) And each shares the same sparse summary treatment. The brown tan canvas shows through – or is left untouched – in many places.

However, Monet has set up a contrast which he was fond of doing in several such pairings. An overcast, 'temps gris', sometimes with rain, would be contrasted with a sunny view of the same motif. Such instances include a pair of garden views at Argenteuil, *Les Lilas, Temps Gris* and *Lilas au Soleil* (W 203-204), and two similarly contrasting views of the port of Le Havre (W 296-297). And Monet might also add variations in lesser compositional elements: here, for example, the foreground boats with figures.

The first owner of this painting was one of Monet's major patrons of the 1870s, a Rumanian homeopath, Georges de Bellio (1828-1894). Several of his Monets are now in the Musée Marmottan, Paris.

156

38. *The Groenburgwal with the Zuiderkerk*, c. 1880. Photo: Amsterdam, Municipal Archives.

34 THE GROENBURGWAL AND THE ZUIDERKERK

Oil on canvas, 54.5 x 65.5 cm
Signed lower right: Claude Monet
W 309
Philadelphia Museum of Art, The W.P. Wilstach Collection, Philadelphia

To illustrate the popularity of this tourist view (see cat. no. 33), another picture is reproduced here (fig. 39).

This painting is clearly a pair with the preceding one (cat. no. 33). Before it was relined in January 1966, the original canvas carried the stamp of Alexis Ottoz, the Paris artist's colourman. For a discussion of their relationship, see the previous entry.

The first recorded owner was the Philadelphia collector, Alexander J. Cassatt, who was much guided in his purchases of Impressionist paintings by his artist sister, Mary Cassatt (1844-1926).

39. Joseph Maximiliaan Kolb and K. Gunkel after Ludwig Rohbock, *View of the Groenburgwal and the Zuiderkerk*. Amsterdam, Municipal Archives.

35 THE MILL 'DE ROOZEBOOM'

Oil on canvas, 54 x 64.8 cm
Signed lower right: Claude Monet
W 302
Houston, The Museum of Fine Arts,
John A. and Andrey Jones Beck Collection

The windmill 'De Roozeboom' at the Onbe-kende Gracht, formerly called 'De Eendracht' or 'Rasphuismolen', was built in 1656. It was a dyewood mill. Redwood, yellowwood and bluewood, cut by convicts of the penitentiary institution of Amsterdam (called Tuchthuis or Rasphuis) into small pieces, were milled between stones. The extract was used to dye textiles. In the 19th century convicts were no longer allowed to do the very hard cutting. The municipality sold the mill in 1828 to a private owner called Rooseboom. It could not stand the fight against the modern chemical paints and was pulled down in October 1876 to make place for the theatre Carré.

The range of colour, the amount of un-touched canvas, and the swift, summary treat-ment clearly connect this painting with those of *The IJ* and *The Montelbaanstoren* (cat. nos. 27 and 28). A date of 1873-74 seems most likely.

This view was one of the most frequently reproduced in a variety of media, and continued to be so even after the windmill was pulled down in October 1876. A stereophotograph of the 1860s can be compared with a painting by P.C. Dommershuizen, and a page from the Guide Conty (figs. 40-42).

The early history of the painting is un-known. Durand-Ruel certainly owned it by 1902, and included it in, or lent it to, several ex-hibitions, where, interestingly, its date was giv-en as 1873.

40. *The mill 'De Roozeboom'*, c. 1870. Stereoscopic view: Amsterdam, Municipal Archives.

41. Pieter Cornelis Dommershuizen, *The mill 'De Rooze-boom'*, c. 1870. Private collection.

On y cultive particulièrement la garance.

Les moulins à vent. — Rien n'étonne les voyageurs visitant la Hollande comme les moulins à vent,

construits avec une profusion telle, que c'est à peine si l'on peut faire deux pas en Hollande sans avoir toujours devant soi un moulin à vent, accessoire obligé de tout paysage hollandais. On les emploie à

42. J. Lemot, *The mill 'De Roozeboom'*. From: *Guide Conty: La Hollande circulaire, guide pratique*, Paris 1884.

161

Oil on canvas, 55 x 65 cm
Signed lower left: Claude Monet
W 300
Private collection

Monet painted this view of the snow-covered Gelderse Kade looking south from a relatively high point, probably from the terrace on the backside of the Schreierstoren. In the distance is the fishmarket; to its left, the Zuiderkerk, to its right the Waag. Compare the modern photograph (fig. 43).

This painting and cat. no. 37 are the only two snowscenes from Monet's Dutch series. In their loose, schematic handling, they are related in date to the other Amsterdam paintings. But without any documentary evidence, it is impossible to say in which month they were painted. Monet produced a magnificent series of snowscapes of Argenteuil in the winter of 1874-75

(W 349-363); it seems likely that the two Amsterdam paintings preceded them.

The first recorded owner of the present picture was Berthe Morisot. She, Monet, Renoir and Sisley held a sale of their work at the Hôtel Drouot, Paris, on 24 March 1875. Berthe Morisot acquired at least one Monet (W 260) from this sale. Could Monet have also presented her with this 'Souvenir d'Amsterdam'?

43. *The Gelderse Kade*. Photo by Menko ten Cate, 1986.

37 THE WESTERDOK AND THE POSTHOORN CHURCH

Oil on canvas, 56 x 73 cm
Signed lower left: Claude Monet
W 301
Present whereabouts unknown

Monet stood on the Westerdoksdijk and looked south towards the Posthoornchurch. Begun in 1863, the church had only one tower when Monet painted it, two further towers not being completed until 1887.

Monet's viewpoint was relatively high. Combined with the diagnolized disposition, this gives his painting compositional analogies with the pair of views of the harbour of Le Havre, executed in January 1874 (W 296 and 297). The loose, schematic handling of this snow-scene is similar to that in Monet's other Amsterdam paintings.

The motif, also taken in winter, was painted in watercolour by the Dutch artist Johan Conrad Greive (1837-1891); but he took his viewpoint from ground-level (fig. 44).

Monet's painting first belonged to the Comte and Comtesse Jean de Rasty, who must have acquired it in the 1870s, together with *The IJ* (cat. no. 27).

164

44. Johan Conrad Greive, *The Westerdok and the Posthoorn Church*. Haarlem, Teylers Museum.

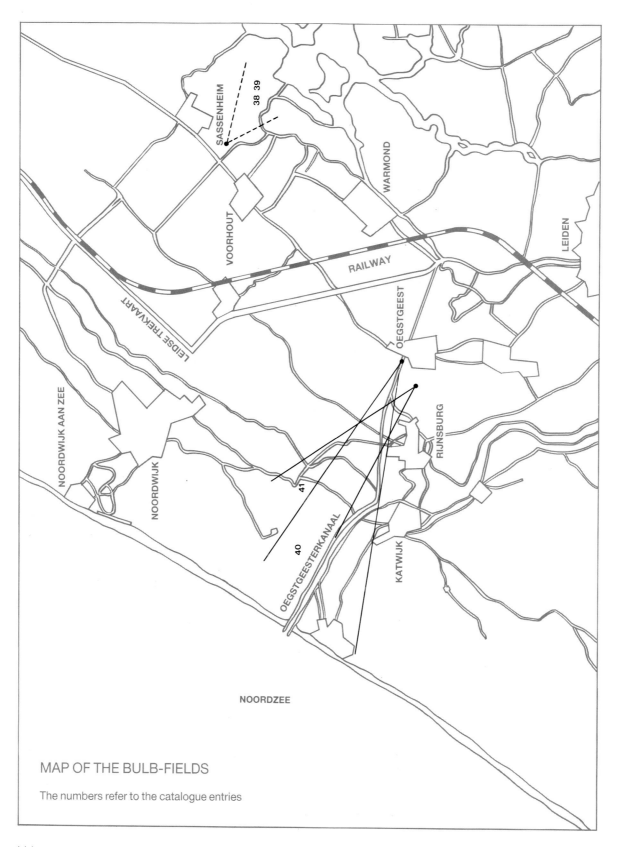

MAP OF THE BULB-FIELDS

The numbers refer to the catalogue entries

The Bulb Fields

Monet's return to Holland in 1886 was by invitation. Writing to Théodore Duret from The Hague on 30 April, he explained: 'I have come here invited by a monsieur whom I did not know, a friend of the Deudons, admirers of my painting (see cat. no. 14), who intended to show me the bulb fields, enormous fields in full flower: they are quite admirable, but drive the poor painter mad: they are unrenderable with our poor colours.'

M. d'Estournelles de Constant, Monet's host, had been at the French legation in The Hague since July 1884. Born in 1852, he had married in June 1885 Daisy Berend, the daughter of a French collector who owned two Monet paintings.

Monet left Paris for The Hague on the evening of Tuesday 27 April and stayed until Thursday 6 May. He travelled alone. His first wife Camille had died in 1879, having given birth to a second son in March 1878. Monet was now living with Alice Hoschedé and her six children at Giverny in Normandy, where they had settled in April 1883. The decade of the 1880s was one of extensive travelling for the artist. Often staying alone for as long as three months at a time, he sought motifs as far apart as the Normandy coast (especially Etretat), the Mediterranean (Bordighera in 1884, Antibes in 1888), a remote island off the coast of Brittany (Belle Isle, 1886), and the Creuse in the Massif Central (1889).

These visits were vividly recorded in the almost daily letters demanded by Alice Hoschedé, the vast majority of which have been preserved. Unfortunately, those Monet must have written from The Hague are lost. His visit to Holland was a brief interlude. Yet during those nine days, he was able to produce five paintings.

The invitation to paint the bulb fields was an intriguing and unusual one. There was almost no tradition, either among Dutch or foreign artists, of depicting them before the last quarter of the nineteenth century. An eccentric painting by Jean-Léon Gérôme of 1882, *The tulip folly* now in the Walters Art Gallery, Baltimore, shows how a latter-day neo-classicist could introduce the flowers into a history-painting. No painter of the Hague School evidently took the slightest interest in using them as a motif; only late in the 1880s and at the beginning of the 1890s, some Dutch artists painted several views of the bulbfields. The first Dutch artist actually to make the flower fields the subject of a painting, was Vincent van Gogh. He did not, however, refer to the painting in his letters. But it is now usually dated to the spring of 1883 when he was living in The Hague. For Van Gogh, this picture was both an exercise in perspective and a bold experiment in colour, enabling him to emancipate himself somewhat from the sombre greys and browns of his Dutch palette (p. 31, fig. 20).

Monet, too, found colour in the bulb fields – sufficient, as he told Duret, 'à rendre fou le pauvre peintre'. And he recalled his impressions to the Duc de Trévise in the 1920s: 'pendant douze jours de suite, j'ai eu à peu près le même temps: quelle bonne fortune! Vous n'aimez pas les champs de tulipes, vous les trouvez trop réguliers? Moi je les admire, et quand on cueille les fleurs avancées, qu'on les entasse et que, tout à coup, sur les petits canaux, on voit comme des radeaux de couleurs, des taches jaunes arrivant dans le reflet bleu du ciel' (Duc de Trévise, 'Le Pèlerinage de Giverny', *Revue de l'Art ancien et moderne* 1927, pp. 126-127).

Monet was mistaken about the number of days he spent in Holland. Furthermore, the weather may not have been as good as Monet remembered. According to the K.N.M.I., the 28th of April was a cloudy day with a light rain; the following day was cold as well, with heavy clouds, rain and storm. Gradually the weather improved; 1st till 6th May it was warm and sunny.

This would seem to suggest that Monet may have begun with the two paintings of motifs taken near Sassenheim (cat. nos. 38, 39), where the skies are slightly overcast; and then continued with the three canvases of the bulb fields and mills near Rijnsburg (cat. nos. 40-42).

While Monet may have been aware of the scientific basis of colour usage and colour perception, his approach was fundamentally empirical and intuitive. By the mid-1880s, however, he had come to doubt the purely 'au premier coup' manner of working that characterised his dozen paintings of Amsterdam (cat. nos. 26-37). Consciously devoted to technical experiment, he felt a need for a more considered working on his canvases, for surfaces that were more substantial. He was torn between observation and reflection; between working directly from nature and finishing his canvases in the studio. He was forty-five years old: an artist's middle period often means retrenchment, reconsideration of his position, self-re-evaluation. Monet was at that stage, between Impressionism and Post-Impressionism, between Realism and Symbolism, between eye and intellect, between perception and conception.

In four of the paintings of bulb fields (cat. nos. 38-41), Monet worked them up away from the motif, partly in Holland, and partly on his return to Giverny. This is especially evident in the Musée d'Orsay canvas (cat. no. 41), where in contrast to the relatively thinly painted sky, the heavily impastoed foreground gives an almost low-relief effect. The Musée Marmottan canvas (cat. no. 42) has not been reworked, and probably shows the extent of Monet's painting session *sur le motif*, thus giving some indication of what the first state of the four other pictures must have looked like.

Less than six weeks after his return from The Hague, Monet included two of his bulb field paintings among the thirteen works exhibited at the 5th *Exposition internationale de peinture* held in the fashionable gallery of Georges Petit. They were quickly sold: one to a Paris stockbroker (cat. no. 38), the other to the daughter of the American millionaire owner of the Singer Sewing Machine Company (cat. no. 41). It seems almost certain that these thirteen paintings were the first Monets to be seen by Vincent van Gogh, recently arrived in Paris in March 1886.

The following year, at the same Georges Petit gallery, Monet hung sixteen paintings, one of which was a *Champs de tulipes, près La Haye* belonging to Boussod, Valadon et Cie. In other words, lent through the aegis of Theo van Gogh. Monet's Dutch connection was now greatly strengthened by his Dutch contact in Paris.

That Monet himself regarded highly his four 'finished' paintings of the bulb fields was affirmed by the fact that he included them all in the large retrospective show, held yet again at the Georges Petit gallery during the Paris International Exhibition of 1889.

Reactions to his bulb fields among French artists and critics were mixed. In a letter of 28 June 1886, J.-K. Huysmans enthused to Odilon Redon: 'Il y a des champs de tulipes en Hollande de Claude Monet, stupéfiants! Une vraie fête des yeux!' But the following year, writing to his son Lucien, on the 15th of May, Camille Pissarro complained of the Stedelijk picture (cat. no. 40), which he had just seen in the company of Bracquemond: 'He (Bracquemond) also noted the crude execution in some of the Monets, particularly in one of the Holland canvases, in which the impasto is so thick that an unnatural light is added to the canvas, you can hardly conceive how objectionable it is to me, – even worse is the swept and meager sky – no, I cannot accept this approach to art.'

Interestingly, Monet's host in The Hague, Baron d'Estournelles de Constant, acquired one of the bulb field paintings (see cat. no. 39). It was his only Monet. There is no evidence that he and Monet ever met again, although Monet corresponded with him in November 1886. By the mid-1890s, the Baron appears to have sold his picture. He lost his Monet, but he maintained his Dutch links. In 1899 and 1907, he represented his country at the International conference of Peace in The Hague. Baron d'Estournelles de Constant was awarded the Nobel Prize for Peace in 1909. He died in 1924.

Jean Léon Gérome, *The tulip folly*. Baltimore, The Walters Art Gallery.

38 BULB FIELDS AT SASSENHEIM

Oil on canvas, 60 x 73 cm
Signed and dated lower left: Claude Monet 86
W 1070
*The Sterling and Francine Clark Art Institute, Williams-
town, Massachussets*

The farm in the centre of this painting probably stood at the southern edge of the village of Sassenheim, at the end of the Knorrenburgerlaan. It was demolished before 1900. Willem van Zonneveld, its proprietor, was a horticulturist.

That the motif was painted at Sassenheim is confirmed by the picture's inclusion in the 5th *Exposition internationale de peinture* at the Galerie Georges Petit, Paris, that opened on 15 June 1886, six weeks after Monet's return from Holland. There, it was catalogued as no. 87 – *Champes de tulipes à Sassenhem (sic) (Hollande)*.

This is probably the first painting of the series of bulb fields. The flowers beyond the small canal in the foreground have not yet been cut, whereas in cat. no. 39 many of them have.

Nonetheless, some cutting of the early blooms has taken place; they float in the water, a phenomenon Monet recalled to the Duc de Trévise almost forty years later: 'suddenly on the small canals, one sees like rafts of colours, yellow stains ('taches') arriving in the blue reflection of the sky.'

The composition is a subtle play of parallel diagonals extending into space from the foreground stretch of water to the farm buildings.

Léon-Marie Clapisson, a Paris stockbroker, acquired the picture, probably at the 1886 exhibition chez Georges Petit. Clapisson owned other works by Monet, as well as Renoir, Sisley and Gauguin.

170

39 BULB FIELDS AT SASSENHEIM

Oil on canvas, 60 x 73 cm
Signed and dated lower right: Claude Monet 86
W 1071
U.S.A., Collection Henry Ford II

Painted on the same size canvas, and identical in motif, this painting is clearly a pair to the preceding one. Monet has here slightly shifted his viewpoint, moving closer to the farm, leaving out the small foreground canal, and looking more to the right.

Stylistically, too, the paintings differ. The refined harmonies of broken colour in cat. no. 38 are here exchanged for a more robust, almost proto-Expressionist handling and colour scheme, especially in the lower third of the canvas, where the tulips have now been cut. And the repeated diagonals have gone, giving a more planar composition. Monet has signed the painting in red, as a deliberate complementary contrast to the predominant green, and as a last touch in the studio.

Appropriately, the first owner of *Bulb Fields at Sassenheim* was Baron d'Estournelles de Constant (1852-1924), who had invited Monet to The Hague expressly to paint the bulb fields. Whether Monet presented it to him or whether he bought it is not known. The Baron lent it to Monet's large retrospective exhibition at the Galerie Georges Petit in 1889, where it was catalogued as no. 94 – *Maison de jardenier; Hollande. 1886*. But evidently it was not with him very long before it crossed the Atlantic to join the enormous collection of Monets amassed by Mrs. Potter Palmer in Chicago.

40 BULB FIELDS AND MILLS NEAR RIJNSBURG

Oil on canvas, 65 x 81 cm
Signed and dated lower right: Claude Monet 86
W 1068
The Hague, Rijksdienst Beeldende Kunst,
on loan to the Stedelijk Museum, Amsterdam.

Monet painted this view, with the dunes silhouetted against a clear sky, just off the Almondeweg. The Almondeweg and the first mill 'De Hoop doet leven', near the Oegstgeesterkanaal, can still be seen from the main road between Amsterdam and The Hague (fig. 45). The second mill 'De Vlinder' was pulled down in the thirties.

Just as cat. nos. 38 and 39 form a pair, so do cat. nos. 40 and 41. Monet has now chosen a larger canvas: 65 x 81 cm. Both paintings have been much worked away from the motif. And since *Bulb Fields and Windmills near Rijnsburg* was not exhibited until May 1887, Monet had more time to contemplate his retouchings in the studio at Giverny. It is now impossible to say which was painted first: and almost irrelevant, because of the extended nature of the execution.

First exhibited at the 6th *Exposition inter-nationale de peinture* at the Galerie Georges Petit, Paris, in 1887 (no. 78), the picture was lent by Boussod, Valadon et Cie – that is, under the aegis of Theo van Gogh. Later, like the *Bulb Fields at Sassenheim* (cat. no. 39), it passed into the collection of Mrs. Potter Palmer of Chicago. In the 1930s, it entered the collection of M.P. Voûte, Jr. the only Dutchman to own any of Monet's paintings of Holland: he also owned *The Blue House on the Hogendijk,* (cat. no. 15).

172

45. *The mill 'Hoop doet leven'.* Photo by H. Bronkhorst, 1986.

41 BULB FIELDS AND MILL NEAR RIJNSBURG

Oil on canvas, 65 x 81 cm
Signed and dated lower left: Claude Monet 86
W 1067
Paris, Musée d'Orsay

In many ways, Monet's paintings of the bulb fields are among the most coloristically vivid he ever did, prefiguring Fauvism and Expressionism. Violent greens, golden yellows, purple-reds and vermillions explode on the canvas. Surfaces are often built up, layer upon layer, almost in low relief, as Monet continued to work out his ideas: this is especially evident in the lower part of the present canvas.

For this painting of the mill 'De Vlinder' and the miller's house Monet moved up a little further on the Almondeweg. Exhibited at the 5th *Exposition internationale de peinture* at the Galerie Georges Petit, Paris in June-July 1886, the painting was bought by the American-born Winnaretta Singer (1860-1943). She married first Comte Louis De Scey-Montbeliard; and secondly in 1893, Prince Edmond de Polignac. Marcel Proust, writing of the Salon of the Prin-cesse de Polignac in *Le Figaro* of 6 September 1903, exclaimed: 'Quelles heures charmantes. Le soleil éclairait en plein le plus beau tableau de Claude Monet que je sache: *Un champ de tulipes près de Harlem.*' The picture was bequeathed to the Louvre in 1943.

42 BULB FIELDS AND MILL NEAR RIJNSBURG

Oil on canvas, 54 x 81 cm
Stamped signature lower left: Claude Monet
W 1069
Paris, Musée Marmottan

Though this particular mill has not been located, the landscape indicates that it is in the neighbourhood of the former two paintings. We are still looking west, in the direction of the dunes, which can be seen in the distance.

This is Monet's fifth painting of the bulb fields. In format it differs from the other two pairs. Loose and schematic, it appears to be carried no further than a preliminary lay-in and hence may show how the 'first state' of cat. nos. 40 and 41 actually looked before their continued reworking.

The painting remained with Monet during his lifetime, and can be seen hanging on the wall, top right, in one of the many photographs taken of his studio (fig. 46).

46. *Monet's studio at Giverny.* From: Exhib. cat. *Monet,* Madrid (Prado) 1986.

SELECTED BIBLIOGRAPHY

General

L. Venturi, *Les archives de l'impressionnisme*, 2 vols., Paris & New York 1939.
John Rewald, *The History of Impressionism*, New York 1973.
Exhib. cat. *A day in the country: Impressionism and the French landscape*, Los Angeles (Los Angeles Museum of Art) 1984.
Exhib. cat. *The New Painting: Impressionism 1874-1886*, Washington (National Gallery of Art) 1986.

Catalogue raisonné

Daniel Wildenstein, *Claude Monet: Biographie et catalogue raisonné*, 4 vols., Lausanne & Paris 1974-1985.

Biographies and monographs

Gustave Geffroy, *Claude Monet, sa vie, son temps, son oeuvre*, Paris 1980 (annotated edition, 2nd issue, Paris 1924).
William C. Seitz, *Claude Monet*, New York, 1960.
Joel Isaacson, *Claude Monet: Observation and Reflexion*, Oxford 1978.
Exhib. cat. *Hommage à Claude Monet (1840-1926)*, Paris (Grand Palais) 1980.
Robert Gordon and Andrew Forge, *Monet*, New York 1984.
John House, *Claude Monet: Nature into Art*, New Haven & London 1986.

Various

Geneviève Aitken and Marianne Delafond, *La collection d'estampes japonaises de Claude Monet à Giverny*, Paris 1983.
Aspects of Monet: A symposium on the artist's life and times, eds. John Rewald and Frances Weitzenhoffer, New York 1984.

Monet in Holland

F. Mars, 'De Franse schilder Claude Monet in Zaandam en Amsterdam', *De Zaende* (1949), pp. 378-82.
F. Mars, 'Claude Monet', *Zaandam 150 jaar stad 1811-1962*, Zaandam 1962, pp. 323-35.
A.H. Huussen jr., 'Claude Monet in Zaandam en Amsterdam in 1871', *Jaarboek Amstelodamum* 66 (1974), pp. 156-64.
A.H. Huussen jr., 'Claude Monet aux Pays-Bas', *Septentrion* 5 (1976), pp. 85-95.
E. van de Wetering, 'Monet langs de snelweg', *Openbaar Kunstbezit/ Kunstschrift* 26 (1982), pp. 75-78.

APPENDIX

I The sketch-book

Paris, Musée Marmottan, inv. no. 5128

Four of Monet's sketch-books are preserved in the Musée Marmottan; one of them contains several drawings executed in Zaandam. It is a worn, almost distintegrated, rectangular book with a bluish green cover, 25.9 cm in height and 34.4 cm in width. Apparently, Monet has used the book all his life. The book contains a drawing from 1865, a composition sketch for his *Déjeuner sur l'Herbe* (which he never finished), but also some pages that should be dated about 1920.

It is as if Monet opened his sketch-book haphazardly each time he wanted to do a sketch, because the sequence of the drawings does not correspond with the dates on which they were created. Consequently, it is hard to get a clear picture of the composition of the sketch-book, also because numerous pages have been cut out. A few of these can be identified from their formats, such as *The Harbour of Fécamp*, reproduced in William C. Seitz' *Claude Monet*, New York 1960, fig. 75.

A notable number of these drawings portray boats and views of harbours. They were partly created in Honfleur, as can be seen from the lettering Ho plus a cipher on the bows and sails of the fishing boats depicted. Moreover, these boats correspond with the kinds of boats Monet painted in Honfleur in the 1860s. Another group is formed by drawings depicting children while reading or writing. These drawings must have been done about 1878-1880, in Giverny, since the children portrayed here are very probably Monet's (step)children.

Some drawings have been executed in red or purple crayon; most of them, however, were done in pencil. Among them are nine drawings that must have been created in Zaandam. Five of them are sketchy views of Zaandam (sheets 32, 34, 31 and 31 bis). Another sketch merely indicates a sailing ship (sheet 31 verso). Monet probably used this sketch for a number of paintings (cat. nos. 11, 21, 24). In this sketch he captured a ship at full speed with a few strokes; in another drawing (sheet 32) he wanted to study the construction and rigging of such ships in detail. Curiously enough, there is a rather primitive rendering of the small house in Zaandam where Czar Peter used to live, and, in another part of the page, awkward sketches of two cows (sheet 34). It makes one wonder if this drawing was not done by someone else, since Monet was a skilful draughtsman.

One of the most interesting drawings in the sketch-book has, up to now, been dated about 1865 (sheet 1; see John House, *Claude Monet: Nature into Art,* New Haven & London 1986, p. 228). In this drawing, two figures – of whom the one to the right is a woman – are vaguely discernible on a balcony or veranda. The picture, showing houses in the background, is cut by a number of vertical bars. Perhaps the narrow vertical shapes represent ship's masts. It is conceivable that this drawing was done from the veranda of a room of Hotel De Beurs. The houses depicted here would consequently, be the houses opposite the harbour. The figure to the right is possibly Monet's wife Camille, while the small, roughly sketched figure to the left may be his four-year-old son Jean.

The functions of the drawings in Monet's sketch-book seem to vary. Some sketches merely contain motifs which are to recur in paintings, such as the mills on the Noordervaldeursloot (sheet 30; cat. no. 10) and the sailing boat (sheet 31 verso; cat. nos. 11, 21, 24). Other drawings appear to be composition sketches. In particular sheet 32, depicting a wooden bridge and houses in the background. Monet has drawn lines along the top and bottom of this sketch, in order to frame the composition. A small sketch portraying dozens of mills and another one with a view of the harbour obviously had that same function (sheets 33 and 31 bis). No paintings were ever done from these sketches, as far as we know. The harbour with its mooring posts, as Monet must have seen it from his hotel, did recur in a painting (sheet 31; cat. no. 1; see House, op. cit., p. 228).

E. v.d. W.

Sketchbook, sheet 1

Sketchbook, sheet 29

Sketchbook, sheet 30

Sketchbook, sheet 31

Sketchbook, sheet 31 verso

Sketchbook, sheet 31 bis

Sketchbook, sheet 32

Sketchbook, sheet 33

Sketchbook, sheet 34

II Letters of Claude Monet

From: Daniel Wildenstein, *Claude Monet: Biographie et catalogue raisonné,* 4 vols., Lausanne & Paris 1974-85, vol. 1, letters nos. 56-59, vol. 2, nos. 671-72.

1. To Camille Pissarro

(London, 27 May 1871), 1 Bath Place Kensington

Mon cher Pissarro,
Après l'état de choses actuel, découragement complet, et, ma foi, nous ne partons pas aujourd'hui.
Soyez donc assez aimable pour nous faire parvenir demain ou après les volumes en question. Si vous venez à Londres, nous y sommes encore tout au moins jusqu'à mardi.
Vous avez appris sans doute la mort de ce pauvre Courbet fusillé sans jugement. Quelle ignoble conduite que celle de Versailles, tout cela est affreux et rend malade. Je n'ai de coeur à rien. Tout cela est navrant.
A vous de coeur,
Claude Monet

2. To the French committee of the International Exhibition in London

Prière de remettre au porteur mes deux marines et leurs cadres.
Zaandam ce 2 juin 71,
Claude Monet

3. To Camille Pissarro

Zaandam ce 2 juin 71

Mon cher Ami,
Nous sommes enfin arrivés au terme de notre voyage, après une assez mauvaise traversée. Nous avons traversé presque toute la Hollande, et certes ce que j'en ai vu m'a paru beaucoup plus beau que ce que l'on dit.
Zaandam est particulièrement remarquable et il y a à peindre pour la vie; nous allons être, je crois, très bien installés. Les Hollandais ont l'air très aimable et hospitaliers.
Nous n'avons pu aller vous serrer la main avant notre départ car j'ai eu pas mal de courses à faire à Londres; j'ai même dû laisser mon affaire de cadres en suspens, et j'espère que, si cela ne vous dérange pas trop, vous voudrez bien encore vous charger d'un petit service pour moi, ce n'est pas très amusant toutes ces commissions, mais, vous le savez, je ne puis m'adresser à d'autres qu'à vous, aussi j'espère que vous ne m'en voudrez pas trop.
Bref, voilà de quoi il s'agit; je n'ai pas fait affaire ni avec le doreur de Brompton Road ni avec Legros, mais, après avoir vu et causé tant bien que mal avec plusieurs doreurs, j'ai trouvé dans le quartier français un doreur qui est tout disposé à acheter mes deux cadres. Mais, comme il n'a pu venir

avec moi à l'internationale voir les susdits cadres avant mon départ, l'affaire en est restée là; mais il m'a donné son adresse que voici: Jos.[h] J.[y] Flack et C. frame manufactory, 21 Green Street, Leicester Square (pardonnez pour mon gribouillage) et il a été entendu avec lui que vous pourriez le voir pour vous entendre et faire l'affaire, c'est-à-dire de lui montrer les cadres, et de me transmettre le prix qu'il offrira (et entre nous, vous pourrez accepter séance tenante son offre si elle n'est pas au-dessous de 8 et même 7 livres) mais attendez son offre; je lui ai parlé de 10 à 12 livres et il n'a pas paru trouver cela cher, seulement je lui avais mes cadres un peu plus cher qu'en réalité, c'est-à-dire 24 livres.
Maintenant, pour lui montrer les susdits cadres, voici ce qu'il vous faudra faire: je suis allé, avant de partir, à l'exposition m'informer s'il était possible de montrer mes cadres; j'ai expliqué mon affaire à Filloneau, et cela se peut très facilement. Il s'agit, pour entrer facilement sans payer, d'aller à l'entrée qui se trouve dans Exhibition Road, la porte la plus près de la station du chemin de fer; et là, demander le bureau de la Commission Française en disant que vous venez pour affaire; Filloneau est prévenu, vous n'aurez qu'à le voir. Faites alors une chose, écrivez au doreur en question qu'il vous donne un rendez-vous, ou bien, si vous allez dans le quartier, voyez-le et entendez-vous.
Je vous envoie ci-joint un mot pour faire enlever mes cadres et les toiles. Maintenant ce doreur avait paru vouloir savoir quel doreur avait fait mes cadres, je ne lui ai pas dit, faites comme moi.
Quant aux toiles, faites-les porter chez Mme. Théobald, j'ai laissé là exprès le bâton pour les rouler. Bien entendu, vous déduirez du prix les dépenses que cela vous causera; mais je vous serais très obligé de me rendre ce service. Ecrivez-moi, dites-moi ce que vous faites et je vous écrirai aussi. Nous sommes complètement sans nouvelles de Paris depuis notre départ de Londres; impossible de se procurer un journal français ici, j'espère en avoir un demain.
Si vous pensez avoir bientôt quelque chose de fini pour mon frère ou mon ami, écrivez-le-moi afin que je les prévienne comme cela a été convenu avec eux. J'espère que ma lettre vous trouvera bien portants tous.
Bébé et ma femme sont très bien après avoir été bien malades en mer. Nous vous envoyons nos bonnes amitiés.
Poignée de main. A vous de coeur,
Claude Monet
Hôtel de Beurs, Zaandam près Amsterdam, Hollande.

4. To Camille Pissarro

Zaandam ce 17 juin (1871)

Mon cher Pissarro,
Je vous demande pardon de ne pas encore avoir répondu à votre première lettre, mais je commence à être dans le feu du travail et n'ai guère de temps. J'ai reçu ce matin même votre seconde lettre et je vois que vous vous donnez bien du mal pour moi et pour n'arriver à rien: je suis au regret de vous donner tant de mal; aussi laissez là cette affaire, je verrai à demander ce service à Durand-Ruel qui pourra peut-être me caser ces maudits cadres.
Je vois que décidément vous allez quitter ce *charmant* pays. Où allez-vous, à Paris ou à Louveciennes? J'espère que vous me l'écrirez.

Quant à nous, nous sommes ici très bien installés et nous resterons là l'été; après, peut-être viendrai-je à Paris, pour le quart d'heure il faut travailler et je suis ici à merveille pour peindre, c'est tout ce que l'on peut trouver de plus amusant. Des maisons de toutes les couleurs, des moulins par centaines et des bateaux ravissants, les Hollandais assez aimables et parlant presque tous le français. Avec tout cela un très beau temps, aussi ai-je déjà mis pas mal de toiles en train.
D'après votre lettre, je vois que vous n'êtes pas si bien partagé que moi et vous n'avez rien pu faire depuis mon départ, cela est bien regrettable, car c'eût été une bonne chose de remporter quelques paysages anglais; enfin, vous allez encore retrouver de belles choses en France, il n'en manque pas non plus là.
Je viens de faire la rencontre de Lévy, le peintre que doit passer quelque temps ici aussi. Je n'ai pas eu le temps de visiter les musées, je veux avant toute chose travailler et je m'offrirai cela après. Adieu, mon cher ami, bon voyage et bonne chance, et n'oubliez pas que vous me ferez bien plaisir en me donnant de vos nouvelles.
Tout à vous. Poignée de mains.
Claude Monet

J'ai oublié, dans ma dernière, de vous dire qu'au moment de quitter Londres nous sommes aperçus que votre neveu avait mis dans le paquet de livres un volume d'Edgar Poe auquel vous tenez, je sais; je l'ai laissé chez Mme Théobald, passez-donc le prendre.
En hâte, tout à vous.
C.M.

Hôtel de Beurs, Zaandam près Amsterdam

5. To Théodore Duret

(The Hague), Légation de France aux Pays-Bas, 30 avril 86

Mon cher Duret,
Je viens de recevoir ici votre lettre. C'est bien aimable à vous d'avoir pensé à moi. Plusieurs fois, je suis passé chez vous, mais toujours lorsque vous veniez de partir. Enfin, nous verrons jeudi prochain.
Je suis venu ici invité par un monsieur que je ne connaissais pas, un ami des Deudon, admirateur de ma peinture, qui tenait à me faire voir des cultures, des champs énormes en pleines fleurs; c'est du rest admirable, mais à rendre fou le pauvre peintre; c'est inrendable avec nos pauvres couleurs.
Toutes les fois que je suis venu à Paris, je me suis muni de votre album, mais je n'ai pas voulu le laisser chez votre concierge, de sorte que je ne pourrai vous le rendre jeudi, car j'arriverai juste d'ici et même peut-être un peu en retard pour notre dîner.
Amitiés et à bientôt.
Tout à vous,
Claude Monet

Chez M. d'Estournelles, Légation de France, La Haye.

6. To A.J. Durand-Ruel

La Haye, 3 mai 1886

Cher Monsieur,
J'ai pu partir pour La Haye sans avoir recours à la proposition que vous m'aviez faite, mais je serais bien aise que vous puissiez m'envoyer de l'argent. Vous devez du reste avoir reçu des nouvelles positives de Monsieur votre père, et de deux choses l'une, où il vous charge de me remettre de l'argent ou bien vous devez me dire que je n'ai plus à compter sur vous.
Enfin faites l'impossible mais envoyez-en-moi par retour du courrier, car il faut que je reparte d'ici jeudi matin au plus tard (plutôt mercredi soir).
Je compte sur une réponse immédiate.
Votre dévoué
Claude Monet

Chez M. d'Estournelles, Légation de France, La Haye.

III Police reports

Correspondence of the Zaandam Commissioner of Police addressed to the Attorney-General at the Courts of Justice in Amsterdam, from June to October 1871, in which Claude Monet is referred to. These reports come from the Zaanstad Municipal Archives; letter-book 1871-1872 of the Zaandam Commissioner of Police.

1.   2 June 1871
To the Attorney-General, commander-in-chief of police for (the province of) North Holland (in) Amsterdam.
Notification is given of the arrival in this city of an alien, one Claude Monet, 31 years of age, a painter, born in Paris. He is presently lodged at the Hotel de Beurs, proprietor Mr. Kellij. Mr. Monet's passport was issued under the Empire and is dated September 5th 1870. He is accompanied by his wife and child, and intends to take up residence here for some time to practise his art. He has travelled from London. Although I have observed noting in connection with the said alien to arouse suspicion, it appeared to me to be an appropriate discharge of my duty to apprise your Honour of this circumstance, which duty I respectfully fulfill herewith.

2. Report for week ending 5 June 1871.
To the Attorney-General for North Holland in Amsterdam.
1. Concerning aliens, nothing to report. (...)
As far as I can ascertain, art. 475, par. 2 is being duly observed in this city.*
I have instructed town and county police constabulary to pay particular attention to aliens who should come here from France. I am having the movements of the foreigner Claude Monet, who has arrived here, closely observed.

*This article of the Penal Code (the Napoleonic *Code Pénal)* directed, in paragraph 2, that innkeepers and landlords should keep a register for the purpose of recording personal information relating to their guests.

3. Report for week ending 19 June 1871.
Attorney-General for North Holland in Amsterdam.
Aliens. To date Claude Monet has done nothing to invite suspicion. (...)

4.   22 June 1871
(To the) Attorney-General for North Holland in Amsterdam.
At the Hotel de Beurs in this town, proprietor Mr. Kellij, two aliens have arrived with the intention of remaining at the said address for some time to come. Their names are Henrij Havard, a merchant, born at Charolles (Soane et Loire), resident in Paris, aged 33, and Henrij Michel Levij, a painter, born and resident in Paris, aged 27. Both are in the possession of foreign passports, the first being dated May 27th 1871, issued by the Préfect du Nord at Lille for Belgium and Holland, the second dated June 6th 1871 and

issued by the French legation in Brussels.
I respectfully apprise you Honour of the residence here of the said persons.

5. Report for week ending 26 June 1871.
Attorney-General for North Holland in Amsterdam.
Aliens. The movements of the Frenchmen previously mentioned as residing here, to wit Monet, Havard and Levij, do not yield anything remarkable. They seek each other's company a great deal, and go for walks or at times row on the Zaan. The two painters are seen working from time to time. (...)

6. Report for week ending 31 July 1871.
Attorney-General for North Holland in Amsterdam.
Aliens. Mr. Levij has returned to France, so that only Mr. Monet with his wife and child still remain in this city. (...)*

*Havard's departure is not documented.

7. Report for week ending 9 October 1871.
Attorney-General for North Holland in Amsterdam.
Aliens. On 8 October the Frenchman Claude Monet, accompanied by his wife and child, left by boat for Amsterdam to continue their journey from there within a few days. (...)

IV Letters of Claude Monet to Theo van Gogh

Amsterdam, Rijksmuseum Vincent van Gogh (Vincent van Gogh Foundation); the letters are translated from the French by Lydia Loader-van den Muyzenberg.

1
Giverny par Vernon eure

Dear Sir,
I hasten to reply to you that the painting which you request-ed from me is yours.
If the frame of the Degas is ready, would you be so kind as to dispatch it to me care of Vernon station as soon as possi-ble, because I have already been waiting a day for it, and then you could have the crate made just large enough for me to return the Belle ile painting in the same case. And I do not think I can come to Paris before the 4th or 5th of May, which will prevent me much to my regret from showing you what I intend to exhibit.
I have much work to do and if I can finish something new, it will only be by working till the last moment.
Therefore could you spare a moment and come to Giverny? Finally, please write to me about the Degas and what I have to do with your painting.
I am delighted that you have sold one of my paintings so quickly and I hope that this will go better and better.
Please accept my sincere regards
Claude Monet
21st april 87

2
Giverny par Vernon eure

Dear Mr. Van gogh,
I am finishing off the two paintings chosen by Mr. Valadon. I shall bring them to you on Monday morning. Shall be with you towards 10 am. please do your best to be there.
Regards
Claude Monet
29th Dec. 88

3
Giverny par Vernon eure

Dear Mr. Van gogh,
Mrs. Hoschedé tells me that you are very sorry about what has happened. Good heavens, I certainly hope that it won't prevent us from doing business together. Moreover, I had not asked to cancel our agreement, I had simply asked Mr. Valadon (and that for my security and peace of mind at the time of my leaving) whether or not he intended to continue fulfilling the said agreement, he gives me back my freedom so it means that these Gentlemen do not wish to continue. I am not at all to blame since on a first occasion at the request of the younger Mr. Boussod I had agreed to his taking only

some of the paintings which I had brought for you. I shall be in Paris tomorrow, and have to leave the same evening for the Creuse. I shall be with you between 11.30 and noon.
I shall like it if we can settle my account with the new paint-ings which have been sold and as I shall also need money, I shall be very glad if of the five or six paintings which you will take from me you will choose two or three from amongst the ones that you already have in your possession and the rest on my return, this would please me and at the same time put matters in order.
till tomorrow then
Yours truly
Claude Monet
5th March 89

4.
Fresselines 25th March (1889)

Dear Mr. Van gogh
I am willing to entrust you for an exhibition in London with those of my paintings which you have, but only if I can be sure of having them for the 10th of May, and with the excep-tion of the view of Belle-ile which you have put aside. As to making a drawing for you, I am so busy with work and I haven't a single thing at hand which I could reproduce, try therefore to do the best you can.
I should also want you to set higher prices in London. Please *tell me* what you intend to do *about this*, and I shall reply at once, because it is the practice in London to put the prices in the catalogue.
I therefore expect to hear from you and at the same time you can let me know which paintings of mine remain. I hope that the new sales have more or less squared my account. I shall be very glad to learn that the balance is in my favour.
please accept my regards
Yours truly
Claude Monet

5.
Hotel du Restaurant de Rome

Garnier
111, Rue St. Lazare
17, Place du Havre
Paris

Dear Mr. Van gogh,
I am leaving in a moment. Will you please wrap the painting with the figures and hand it to the bearer. Since Mr. Faure has not completely devarnished his he has not sent it to you.
Regards
Claude Monet
7th June 89

6.
Giverny par Vernon eure
10th July 90

Dear Mr. Van Gogh,
I have not replied to your letter at once because I was not sure to be here on the 14th of July and because I waited to be certain myself before letting you know.

If therefore you wish to inform Mr. Valadon about it, I ask you to postpone your visit until August, that will be better in every respect because with this appalling weather we're having work is going badly and I am anxious to show you something other than unfinished attempts. Moreover I am a little short of paintings. Mr. Durand-Ruel having bought several from me. I shall let you know when I have interesting things to show you, if the weather starts to improve it will be earlier than I think.
please accept my regards
cordially yours Claude Monet

I have recently had a visit from Mr. La Rochefoucauld who told me that he has bought from you the pine-tree on the Mediterranean coast, which pleased me. That is one at least which has the good fortune not to go to America.
C.M.

7.
Giverny par Vernon eure
15th August 90

Dear Mr. Van Gogh,
I beg you to excuse me. I wanted every day to offer you my condolences on the misfortune which has befallen you but I am working so frantically that I am outside from 4 in the morning and only go to home for my meals and am so engrossed that I forget everything else.
I'm sure you will excuse me and believe how much I was affected on your behalf by such a loss. I have told you what I thought of your brother, it's a double misfortune for you.
Please accept my kindest regards
and I remain
entirely yours
Claude Monet

8.
Giverny par Vernon eure
7th Oct. 90

Dear Mr. Van Gogh,
I shall be very glad to know if you have informed these Gentlemen of our conversation and what are their intentions. I should quite like to close my account and reach an agreement concerning the few paintings which you still have and in which I am interested.
Would you kindly write to me about this. As I have told you, I had a visit from Mr. Durand-Ruel who has bought about ten of my canvases from different periods, four of which were done this year. So if Mr. Valadon makes up his mind to come with you, you will be able to see quite a few new things, especially as I am very much in the mood for work at the moment. In any case let me know the intentions of these gentlemen. I hope that with this fine weather you have been able to recover from your indisposition.
Yours truly
Claude Monet

PHOTOCREDITS